Insight Text Guide

Virginia Lee BA(HONS),Dip.Ed.

Lantana

Directed by Ray Lawrence

Insight Publications

First published in 2004.

Insight Publications Pty Ltd
ABN 57 005 102 983
128 Balcombe Road
Mentone
Victoria 3194
Australia.
Tel: 61 3 9583 5839
Fax: 61 3 9583 9573
Email: books@insightpublications.com.au

www.insightpublications.com.au

Cover Design: Graphic Partners
Internal Design: Sarn Potter
DTP: SPG
Series Editor: Robert Beardwood
Editing: Dianne Bramich, Jacinta Watson
Printed by Hyde Park Press, South Australia

National Library of Australia Cataloguing-in-Publication data:
Lee, Virginia.
Lantana – Ray Lawrence.
For senior secondary English students.
ISBN 1 920693 56 4.
1. Lantana (Motion picture). I. Title.
791.4372

contents

CHARACTER MAP

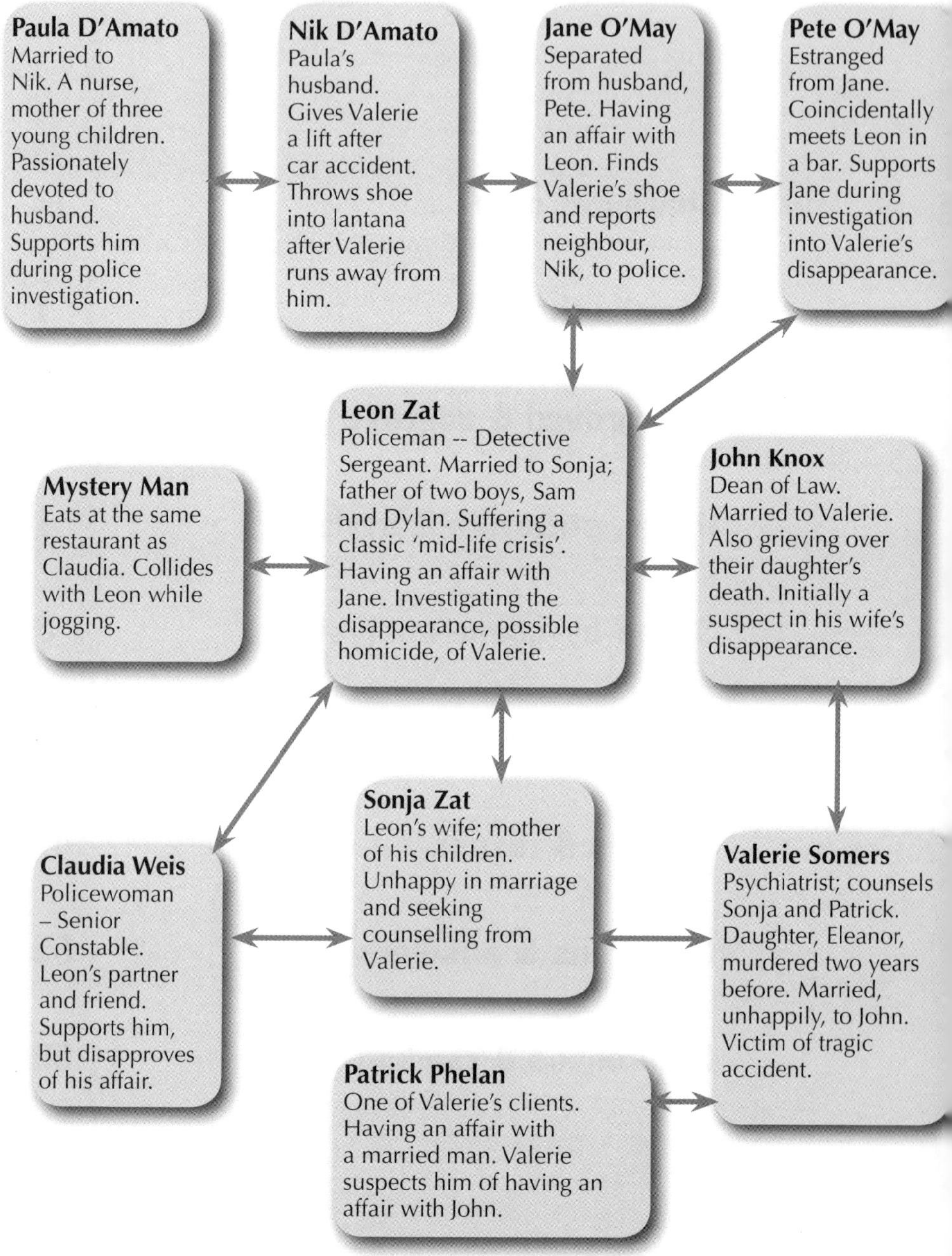

Paula D'Amato
Married to Nik. A nurse, mother of three young children. Passionately devoted to husband. Supports him during police investigation.

Nik D'Amato
Paula's husband. Gives Valerie a lift after car accident. Throws shoe into lantana after Valerie runs away from him.

Jane O'May
Separated from husband, Pete. Having an affair with Leon. Finds Valerie's shoe and reports neighbour, Nik, to police.

Pete O'May
Estranged from Jane. Coincidentally meets Leon in a bar. Supports Jane during investigation into Valerie's disappearance.

Leon Zat
Policeman -- Detective Sergeant. Married to Sonja; father of two boys, Sam and Dylan. Suffering a classic 'mid-life crisis'. Having an affair with Jane. Investigating the disappearance, possible homicide, of Valerie.

Mystery Man
Eats at the same restaurant as Claudia. Collides with Leon while jogging.

John Knox
Dean of Law. Married to Valerie. Also grieving over their daughter's death. Initially a suspect in his wife's disappearance.

Sonja Zat
Leon's wife; mother of his children. Unhappy in marriage and seeking counselling from Valerie.

Claudia Weis
Policewoman – Senior Constable. Leon's partner and friend. Supports him, but disapproves of his affair.

Valerie Somers
Psychiatrist; counsels Sonja and Patrick. Daughter, Eleanor, murdered two years before. Married, unhappily, to John. Victim of tragic accident.

Patrick Phelan
One of Valerie's clients. Having an affair with a married man. Valerie suspects him of having an affair with John.

INTRODUCTION

Lantana is a psychological drama that explores the vulnerabilities and strengths that underpin contemporary relationships. Its complex, interwoven plot examines four marriages within the context of a missing person's investigation, each one of which is dealing with its own specific challenges and heartaches. The film is 'part mystery, part thriller and part journey through the labyrinth of love'.[1]

Lantana was produced by Jan Chapman and directed by Ray Lawrence, and was only Lawrence's second feature film, the first being the quirky adaptation of Peter Carey's novel, *Bliss* (1985). Despite the acclaim of this film, Lawrence returned to his lucrative career in advertising, directing television commercials, while he waited for the next engaging project. *Lantana*'s screenplay was written by Andrew Bovell and adapted from his stage play, *Speaking in Tongues*, which was first performed in Sydney in 1996. When Lawrence saw the play, despite its theatricality, he recognised its filmic potential and he, Chapman and Bovell collaborated closely on the ensuing adaptation.

Lawrence gathered together a talented ensemble of Australian actors, including Anthony LaPaglia, Geoffrey Rush and Kerry Armstrong. The casting represents an effective balance between well-known 'names' with an international profile and locally based actors often playing 'against type'. With an evocative musical score by well-known songwriter, Paul Kelly, and stylish cinematography by Mandy Walker, the film is a beautifully realised production with a distinctive Australian quality.

Lantana was the most successful Australian film of 2001, both commercially and critically, winning seven of the major Australian Film Institute awards: Best Film, Best Director, Best Actor, Best Supporting Actor, Best Actress, Best Supporting Actress and Best Adapted Screenplay. It premiered at the 2001 Sydney Film Festival and was also screened at the Melbourne and Brisbane Film Festivals, before its general Australian release in October of that year. It was subsequently showcased at the Toronto International Film Festival where it received rave reviews: '...this flawless Australian masterpiece...is a sublime achievement, understated in its cinematic direction, a work in which the substance of character rises to the top'.[2]

---

[1] Andrew Bovell, *Lantana* Screenplay, Currency Press, Sydney, 2001, p.11.

[2] P. Fischer, *filmmonthly.com* http://www.palace.net.au/lantana/reviews.htm

BACKGROUND & CONTEXT

Lantana is set in the present in the familiar urban landscape of Sydney. The context will be immediately recognisable to Australian students and, as such, a study of the text does not require a great deal of background information.

Sydney

Sydney is the largest city in Australia, the capital of New South Wales, and the site of first white settlement in this country. It is a sophisticated metropolis with a population of approximately four million people. Its already high international profile was further enhanced when it hosted the very successful 2000 Olympic Games. Intensive media coverage showcased the spectacular natural beauty of the harbour and familiar icons like the Sydney Opera House and the Sydney Harbour Bridge. Sydney's suburban sprawl is extensive. Like any large city, there are attendant social problems and there is reference, in the text, to illicit drug trafficking. As a policeman, Leon often deals first-hand with the downside of urban living.

Australian Society

The characters depicted in *Lantana* represent a cross-section of Australian society and, collectively, their experiences encompass a broad and detailed portrait of Australian life. As a senior policeman, supporting a family, Leon falls into the medium socioeconomic range. He and Sonja live in inner suburban Sydney in a renovated Victorian cottage. Jane, Nik and Paula live further out in the suburbs. The fact that there is a vacant block opposite their house overgrown with lantana suggests a less built-up neighbourhood. Jane's house, a conventional brick veneer, towers over Nik and Paula's small bungalow. It is evident from their house – which is modest and not particularly well maintained – that the young couple do not have a great deal of disposable income. This is further illustrated by Jane's reference to their precarious financial state. Nik is unemployed and looks after his youngest child at home. Paula's income as a nurse supports their family of five. By contrast, John and Valerie represent the professional middle class. The joint income of a senior academic and a psychiatrist delivers all the trappings of an affluent lifestyle: a beautiful architect-designed home in a

North Shore bush setting complete with coastal view, the opportunity to dine out regularly, and so forth. They commute into the city on a day-to-day basis, as do many who live in Sydney's outer suburbs.

Lantana also depicts a postmodern cultural landscape and explores the way in which traditional institutions, such as marriage and family, are being reviewed. It questions the relevance and viability of the conventional frameworks of the past, and suggests that if these are to endure they must be sustained by certain core values. The traditional institutions of marriage and the nuclear family are not inviolate, nor do they have a monopoly in terms of producing successful relationships. The film demonstrates that these structures will not survive simply because they have done so up until now. *Lantana* contrasts nuclear families, whose children range from preschoolers to teenagers. Sonja and Leon, Nik and Paula may be at different stages of parenting, but their lives together are based on a concept of community that transcends the individual. We also see couples without children, though even here there is no set model. Whereas John and Valerie's childlessness has come about through tragedy, Jane and Pete's may simply be a lifestyle choice. Finally, the alternative of gay love is touched on in the film. None of these options are presented as being inherently preferable; the only value judgments being made are on the basis of the commitment and particular qualities that each party brings to the relationships.

Lantana

According to the *Oxford English Dictionary*, lantana is 'a genus of tropical shrub with small colourful blooms that hides a dense, thorny undergrowth'. It grows profusely around Sydney. Within the text, lantana is employed as a metaphor for the intricate web of relationships explored throughout. The lives of eleven individuals connect and intersect in a complicated fashion, evoked at the outset by the epigraph promoting the drama: 'It's tangled'. The motif also represents the profound complexity of love itself: its possibilities, its permutations, its dense emotional threads. The film examines issues such as betrayal, loyalty, obsession, desire, suspicion and jealousy, and provides few easy answers to the question of how people can love happily. Like the lantana scrub, love is beautiful, fragile and dangerous. In adapting his original script for the screen, Andrew Bovell decided to find a new title that 'symbolically…gave the sense of a new beginning'. He explains:

> To me the lantana vine visually manifested the inter-weaving and mysterious nature of the story I was trying to tell. It's an impenetrable vine with twisted and entangled branches that conceal a dark interior. It's covered in exquisite and delicate flowers but when you reach in to pick one, your hand is cut to shreds by hundreds of tiny thorns. These qualities find their expression in the structure of the story.[3]

Throughout the text, the image of lantana keeps reasserting itself. A common thread is the way in which lantana hides secrets: the mystery of the woman's body at the beginning, the children's game of 'hide and seek', and Valerie's shoe. When Jane is looking for the latter, she hides from Nik in the thick undergrowth of the vine. Ultimately, when the mystery of Valerie's disappearance is resolved, the lantana yields up its secrets as, literally, her corpse is winched up to safety.

GENRE, STRUCTURE & STYLE

Genre

Lantana, like many contemporary films, is a multi-generic text. Not only are several genres combined, it is also worth noting the way in which the text repeatedly and skilfully shifts focus. Audience expectations are foiled as different elements are synthesised to create a complex whole.

Lantana's opening suggests a conventional thriller. The disturbing beginning – with its blackouts, sinister music, claustrophobic sense of tragedy and, of course the bloodied lifeless victim – establishes the fact that here is a mystery that needs to be solved. However, the film quickly evolves into an acutely observed character study, a taut drama, scrutinising contemporary marriage. Four relationships are put under the microscope and the various issues that each couple confront come to the fore. We are introduced to Leon and Sonja, whose marriage is under threat: Leon is having an extramarital fling while his wife, who does not know of his infidelity, is seeking counselling. Her therapist is Dr Valerie Somers whose own relationship with her husband, John, has been profoundly compromised by the tragedy of their young daughter's murder two years before. Two other couples, Jane and Peter, and their neighbours, Nik and Paula, are also drawn into the narrative. The focus, at this stage, is the emotional dynamic between the protagonists. When Valerie disappears on

[3] Bovell, *Lantana* Screenplay, p.10.

her way home from work one evening and Leon is assigned to investigate the case, the film reverts to a missing person's investigation, though it still retains its introspective edge. The familiar elements of a police drama – interrogations, follow-up leads, a classic denouement (disentangling of the plot) with the suspect confessing the truth – are all incorporated into the meld. However, there is also a second denouement that ties up all the emotional threads; the closing montage illustrates this well as it presents us with the respective outcomes of the key players.

Structure

Structurally, *Lantana* is complex. In writing the script, Andrew Bovell has acknowledged his creative debt to the multi-narrative films of Robert Altman and films such as *Happiness* (Todd Solondz) and *Magnolia* (Paul Thomas Anderson). Having expressed his dissatisfaction with 'narratives that [have] focused on the journey of a single protagonist', Bovell has instead sought to explore the way in which 'different points of view might glean quite different and sometimes contrary meaning from the same incident'. He comments:

> I was interested in finding new narrative shapes…I wanted to work on a lateral plane rather than a linear one. I was interested in the random connections between people and how we make sense of our own lives through encountering the lives of others.[4]

Valerie's disappearance is the catalyst that drives the story-line. 'It is like a stone dropped into a still pond, the ripples circling out and affecting all that they touch.'[5] The text commences with reference to her death and then goes back to explore the sequence of events that led to the accident. This convention is typical of the detective or mystery genre, though in *Lantana*'s case, as has been noted, we then detour into more emotional territory.

The plot is character-driven, with a number of interacting narrative threads:

- Sonja and Leon's marital dilemma
- Leon's relationship with Jane
- Jane's estrangement from Pete
- Eleanor's murder and its impact on her parents
- The police investigation into Valerie's disappearance

---

[4] Bovell, *Lantana* Screenplay, p.9.

[5] Bovell, *Lantana* Screenplay, p.10.

- Nik's complicity in the case and its effect on his relationship with Paula
- Claudia and her mystery man's blossoming rapport
- Patrick's affair with his married lover and the way this impacts on Valerie.

While these plot lines converge, there are few clichés and no resolute endings. The unpredictability and messiness of people's lives, accurately charted by the film, makes it impossible for things to be tied up too nea tly.

Style

Cinematically, *Lantana* is naturalistic in style. Lawrence has deliberately used a visual production style designed to complement the contemporary story being told. His stated agenda shuns an overtly contrived approach: 'The more things that you can get rid of, the simpler I can make it, the better. That's my theory, my process.'[6] For example, only natural light was used in the filming and the lack of artificial lighting, though difficult from a technical perspective, enhanced the actors' freedom to deliver realistic performances. Cinematographer Mandy Walker explains that Lawrence believes not so much in creating a mood, but 'in the mood already being there in the location, and so it was about capturing that'.[7] This strategy of utilising the inherent potential of a given location or set, as opposed to creating a simulated atmosphere, gives the film a particularly authentic texture.

Reading Film as Text

Lantana is a non-print text and, as such, students must refer to film language and the particular qualities that characterise the genre. While there are elements common to all texts – characters, themes, and so forth – there are also features specific to cinema. How do the images on the screen create meaning? How do added components, such as the soundtrack, reinforce the underlying concerns of the text?

Students are expected to have an understanding of the different *camera shots* and *angles*, and ask themselves what choices have been made, and why. In the study of film the camera work is just as instrumental, in terms of informing the narrative, as character-driven action and dialogue. *Long shots*

[6] *Lantana* Press Kit, Beyond Films, Sydney, 2001, p.9.

[7] *Lantana* Press Kit, p.10.

traditionally establish location and set the context; for example, in *Lantana* they are used to differentiate between the different Sydney locales – inner suburban, coastal bushland – and provide visual clues about which subplot is taking centre stage. *Medium shots*, the most common, show aspects of a scene and *close-ups* are typically used for more intimate moments between characters. These are employed to great effect in *Lantana*. For example, Lawrence uses *extreme close-up shots* when Valerie and John are making love; the camera focuses directly on their faces and we are able to read the raw ambivalence and sense of personal isolation that each brings to the act. *Tracking* and *panning shots* direct the audience to follow a specific course, while a *zoom shot* isolates detail by 'zeroing in' from a wide angle, or long shot, to a close-up in one continuous movement.

Furthermore, the *placement of the camera* is a relevant consideration. Shooting a character from above or below can alter our perception of the situation they are in and may suggest either empowerment or the opposite. For example, the *overhead shot* of John's car, parked in the laneway where his daughter's body was found, emphasises his disempowerment and the fact that his life has been robbed of choice. Note also the *framing* (visual composition) within the scenes – the ways in which people or objects are arranged. In *Lantana*, Lawrence often positions his characters sitting opposite each other, or side by side in cars, as they attempt to interact with each other. Consider the effect of this positioning.

Mise en scène (a French term meaning 'scene setting') refers to the visual and design elements of a film. Literally everything we see on the screen – locations, sets, background details, costumes, even the use of colour and lighting – has been deliberately selected and is encoded with meaning. When Valerie leaves her messages on the fateful night of the accident, the two photographs on the phone table – one of her and Eleanor, and another of her and John smiling into the camera – are a poignant reminder of the way that grief has ripped this family apart. Another interesting example is the backdrop used in the scene where Jane manipulates a meeting with Leon. They stand in front of a large billboard featuring a child's face; her eyes are positioned between their two figures, silently rebuking their clandestine flirtation.

It is worth noting the continual play of contrasts in the film. The colour and animation of the Salsa club is juxtaposed against the lonely, dark road of Valerie's last drive; the warm bustle and mellow, welcoming tones of the Zats' home contrast sharply with the monochromatic sterility of Valerie's consulting rooms. Most of *Lantana*'s scenes are filmed indoors and many of them are shot at night. A technique that Lawrence deploys regularly throughout the text is the way that the screen morphs into black – the chilling opening, Valerie's last night – a device designed to evoke a sense of menace and generate suspense. The use of natural lighting has already been acknowledged. The characters can be 'exposed' by bright sunlight as the disparity between their aspirations and the reality of their lives is revealed; for example, Valerie lying alone in the marital bed the morning after she and John have had intercourse. Alternatively, bright light celebrates. The scenes of Nik and Paula, together with their young family, are invariably brightly lit, like the final scene in the garden, which highlights their solidarity and contentment.

Editing, the way in which each scene is constructed and then juxtaposed against the next to create a meaningful sequence, is a key element of the film-making process. Joining shots and scenes together links them in the audience's mind, either in terms of the narrative itself or thematically. In *Lantana*, the scenes are short and briskly edited, and the continual shifts emphasise the fractured nature of the lives being examined. *Montage* is a series of very short scenes or shots, often set to music – a rapid editing of images that form a kind of cinematic collage. Montage is used effectively at the end of the film to succinctly tie together the various narrative threads and provide some sense of closure.

SCENE-BY-SCENE ANALYSIS

The segmentation featured follows the segmentation of the DVD version of the film.

Segment 1: Opening Credits

Scene 1) Opening Credits. Exterior. Day. The names of the key players are superimposed over a backdrop of lantana – thick, tangled and in blossom – while the soundtrack features the insistent hum of cicadas. The camera slowly pans into a black space in the centre of the bush. Immediately a sense of disquiet is established, and the subsequent blackout suggests sinister deeds afoot. A single ominous chord heralds the return of the scene as the close-up shot reveals a woman's bloodied foot, shoeless, inert. Flies buzz around the wound. The camera follows the line of the woman's leg until the whole corpse is revealed. She is lying on her stomach, face down, with one arm twisted awkwardly behind her back. Her skirt is hiked up. It is unclear whether her death is accidental or she is a victim of foul play. The scene fades to another blackout, leaving the mystery unresolved.

Scene 2) Motel. Interior. Day. Jane and Leon are in bed together, having passionate sex. This is followed by the rather prosaic contrast of getting dressed. Jane searches for her lost earring and Leon's offer to help elicits the rueful admission that she is particularly fond of them as they were a gift from her husband. This disclosure and the accompanying sheepish exchange reveal the illicit nature of their relationship. While each acknowledge that they 'really enjoyed' their time together, the framing of the scene – the pointed distance between them across the bed – and the subsequent coy kiss goodbye suggest that genuine intimacy is not a feature of the affair.

Scene 3) Leon's Car. Day. As Leon drives away, he finds the earring ironically ensnared in the crotch of his pants. He puts it in his pocket.

Q Note the mise en scène. The dark tunnel through which Leon drives as he leaves the rendezvous with his lover to join his wife is a recurring image in the text. What might it mean in the context of this scene?

Scene 4a) Dance Studio. Exterior. Dusk. Leon meets his wife, Sonja, who is waiting for him outside the dance studio. She waves, obviously pleased to see him.

Scene 4b) Dance Studio. Interior. Evening. The Zats watch the salsa being performed. However, it is clear from their body language that while Sonja is engaged by the infectious rhythm, Leon is there under sufferance. His awkwardness is compounded by the appearance of Jane who also learns at the studio. Leon's lack of enthusiasm on the dance floor frustrates the dance instructor who finally intervenes to partner Sonja himself. The intimation that Leon does not appreciate his wife's sexuality is played out in front of an audience that includes his lover and, obviously, has a wider application than just this particular context. The camera moves from Jane's sympathetic close-up to Leon's glowering discomfort, while his positioning off centre screen further highlights his marginalisation from the rest of the group.

Q Why do you think Leon has agreed to attend the dance class?

Segment 2: Why Are You Jogging, Dad?

Scene 5) Hill Outside Zats' House. Exterior. Morning. An overhead shot of Leon as he jogs doggedly up the hill to his house. His breathing is so laboured that he has to stop, winded, as a neighbour looks on.

Scene 6) Zats' Kitchen. Interior. Morning. Inside the house, Sonja and the boys get ready for work and school. Overall, the scene depicts a typical family dynamic. Leon is demonstrative to his sons and insists that the reluctant Sam kisses him goodbye.

Scene 7) Drug Bust. Interior. Day. Leon, his partner Claudia, and other members of the police squad break into the home of a drug dealer. Leon is extremely aggressive – repeatedly kicking a suspect as he lies on the floor.

Scene 8) Leon's Car. Day. As Claudia and Leon watch the suspects being led away, it is clear that the violence has disturbed Claudia. She queries Leon's tactics: 'You went in a bit hard'. He reveals a zero tolerance for those who deal in drugs, calling them 'scum' and implying that they deserve everything they get. His response may also be symptomatic of stress.

Scene 9) Police Station. Interior. Day. As Leon and Claudia sit opposite each other at the police station, completing their paperwork, Leon enquires if she is 'seeing anyone'. Her negative response highlights her single status and the difficulties of maintaining a relationship, given the demands of her job. Her jibe that 'male cops are lousy in bed' defuses the tension between them. She admits to Leon that she has exchanged shy glances with a man who eats at the same restaurant as she does and that 'it's a start'. Good humour restored, Claudia asks to be remembered to Sonja. While the conversation demonstrates the camaraderie between the partners, it also suggests that Leon and his wife are spending less time together. As if to corroborate this, we hear Valerie's voice-over: 'Have you told him you're not happy?'

Key Scene

Scene 10) Valerie's Consulting Rooms. Interior. Day. Sonja is in a counselling session. It is a source of frustration and distress to her that Leon seems to have no sense of her true feelings. When Valerie asks her how does she want her marriage to be, Sonja replies, 'Passionate and challenging and honest'. She refutes the idea that their relationship is 'emotionally honest' and confesses that she and Leon are merely 'going through the motions'. It is clear she wants more. While Valerie is sympathetic, she is also passive and detached – the therapist's role. The two women are a study in grey. They sit silhouetted against a stark backdrop of pale neutrality that provides an unforgiving foil to Sonja's revelations, and emphasises their respective emotional isolation.

Q Are Sonja's expectations too high given what we have seen of Leon's behaviour?

Q What do you think she means by 'emotionally honest'?

The early scenes establish the theme of marriage in crisis. Leon and Sonja, on the face of it, maintain a conventional domestic facade and present a united front to outsiders. Their two sons seem unaware of any dissension between their parents. Arguably, as a couple, they are in fact doing more than just 'going through the motions'. For example, despite Leon's reluctance, they *do* attend the dance class together. Yet there are obvious tensions simmering beneath the surface. Leon is unfaithful to his wife and Sonja is in therapy. While both these responses are expressions of discontent and unhappiness, there is no evidence at this point that either is clued into the actions of the other, or specifically reacting against their partner. Rather, each is independently responding to the discontent itself. It is worth noting the difference in their respective 'strategies'.

Segment 3: The Book Launch

Scene 11) Bus Stop. Exterior. Day. As Valerie waits for her taxi, she catches the eye of a little schoolgirl. This evokes a wistful memory of the daughter who, it emerges, died at about the same age.

Key Scene

Scene 12) Book Launch. Interior. Evening. Valerie has published a book about her daughter, Eleanor, who was murdered two years before at the age of eleven. As she acknowledges the applause of the audience, her husband John hurries up the stairs to join the gathering. He passes a large poster of their daughter, advertising the book launch. Valerie commences by speaking generally of a prevailing and corrosive disillusionment within the community. 'We don't know what to feel any more. We don't know what's right or wrong any more.' The oracles of a more innocent age, government leaders, priests, parents, no longer suffice. The concept of family has broken down. Home is 'a sanctuary' for 'the privileged few' only: 'for most it's a battleground'. As she addresses her audience, the camera shoots her from behind, through a fluttering gauze curtain, as if to emphasise the ephemeral nature of the qualities she is referring to. She asks rhetorically, 'Can we believe in love? Feel safe in it?' As she refers to love, she looks questioningly at her husband. She concludes, 'Loving someone means we have to relinquish power…It's mutual surrender'. At this point, the camera focuses on another man, Patrick, who also listens sceptically. Note the music change for the cut to Patrick.

Valerie's assertion that 'Trust is as vital to human relationships as breathing is to life – and just as elusive' raises one of the key issues of the text. The idea that relationships cannot sustain dishonesty has direct implications for Leon and Sonja. While Leon's infidelity is threatening his marriage, lying about it is even more damaging. And although Sonja does not know the full extent of his deception, she senses the lack of openness in their partnership and resents it enough to seek professional counselling. Equally, it becomes clear that Valerie and John's own marriage is weighed down by lack of communication. We have the sense of another couple whose lives are running along parallel tracks with no converging agenda. Valerie's address also points to the difficulties of maintaining faith in a predominantly cynical society. She refers to 'the confused cry of the modern age'. People want to believe in something and they need the security of responsible authority figures. But, increasingly, the icons of the past can no longer be trusted either. This lack of trust in terms of the broader context throws the weight of expectation even more onto personal relationships, though, at the same time, ill equips individuals to nurture their loved ones appropriately. Note her continual refrain, 'It's not meant to be like that'. 'This wasn't supposed to happen.'

Scene 13) John's Car. Night. As John and Valerie drive home, the conversation is stilted. He comments that the launch seemed to go well. She confides that she was worried he wouldn't make it. He reiterates that he had made the commitment and, in an attempt to reassure her, takes her hand. Nevertheless, the silence between them is not a comfortable one.

Scene 14) Knoxs' House. Interior. Night. Valerie lights the candles in front of Eleanor's photograph in what is clearly a nightly ritual. Note here the cut from Eleanor's framed photograph to Valerie's framed face in the mirror. John offers Valerie a whisky, which she declines on the basis that she has an early client in the morning. He then suggests it would be more convenient to take separate cars to work the following day, but she insists that she does not mind waiting for him. Once again, the dialogue between them suggests cross-purpose. John complies with her desire to drive together, but the intimation is that he would have preferred to go alone. The framing of each – to the far left in Valerie's case and the far right in John's – emphasises the divide between them. Equally, the lingering shot of Valerie standing in the half-light before her daughter's picture underscores her emotional estrangement.

Scene 15) Valerie's Consulting Rooms. Interior. Day. Patrick tells Valerie of the casual sexual encounter which has turned into something more meaningful. He admits that he likes this man 'very much', but he 'comes encumbered with a wife'. Patrick clearly resents his lover's divided loyalties and is critical of the wife who may be deceiving herself. Valerie seems to find it difficult to empathise with the position he takes.

Q Take note of the camera angles in this scene. How do they contribute to its meaning?

Segment 4: Get His Number?

Scene 16a) Suburban Exterior. Day. The camera pans slowly over a thick expanse of lantana in bloom. The image evokes the opening scene. A long shot over the bush reveals two houses; one is Jane's, the other belongs to her neighbours, Nik and Paula. This scene is intercut with:

Scene 16b) Jane's House. Interior. Day. Jane looks down through her window at Nik as he works on the car, and practises her dance routine to an up-tempo Latin rhythm. This reverts to:

Scene 16c) Nik and Paula's Garden. Exterior. Day. Jane comes down to join Paula and her young daughter in their front garden. She flirts with Nik and then sits down with Paula. The companionship between the two women is evident as they pick up a conversation regarding Jane's love life. Jane reveals that the man she has slept with is married and presumably unhappy. Paula relays the information that Nik has met Jane's own estranged husband, Pete, who wants to return home, but Jane argues that she doesn't love him. Obviously she is the one who has initiated the separation. While Paula is supportive of her neighbour, she also intuitively disapproves of any marriage being threatened by an outside party. Moreover, their friendship will be compromised by Jane's too obvious interest in Nik.

The conversations between Valerie and Patrick and Jane and Paula are mirror images of each other. In both cases, the 'other party' is disclosing an illicit relationship with a married man. Each rationalise their actions. Both are dismissive of the impact these actions might have on the families in question.

Q We only view Patrick's affair from the outside. Does Leon and Jane's relationship invite any more sympathy, given that we are offered greater insight into the respective situations of these two characters?

Scene 17) Street. Exterior. Night. Jane waits in her car outside the police station. When Leon comes out with Claudia, she engineers a meeting. After an awkward introduction, Claudia excuses herself and Leon asks how Jane has been. He returns her earring.

Q Consider the effect of the mise en scène. What might the child's unblinking stare suggest?

Scene 18) Restaurant. Interior. Night. Claudia finishes her meal and reluctantly leaves the restaurant. As she walks away, the man she has been hoping to see enters the same restaurant and sits down. She watches him through the window, her disappointment obvious.

Q Claudia's quest for love is contrasted against the challenged or failing relationships that surround her. What is its purpose in the film?

Scene 19a) Nik and Paula's House. Exterior. Night. Nik returns from walking the baby. He notes the car parked in front of Jane's house.

Scene 19b) Nik and Paula's Kitchen. Interior. Night. Nik tells Paula of the unmarked police car outside and asks if Jane is seeing a cop.

He is angry and feels compromised as Pete, Jane's husband, is 'a mate'. Paula advises him to 'stay out of it'.

Q What does it suggest about Nik's background that he can recognise an unmarked police car?

Scene 20) Jane's House. Interior. Night. Leon and Jane are again having sex. To her concern and alarm, he collapses with chest pain. When she contends that he should have told her he had 'a weak heart', Leon angrily insists he is fine. He also denies that they are, in fact, having a relationship. 'This is not an affair. It's a one night stand, except it happened twice!' He subsequently apologises. She hugs him.

Q How does Leon view his liaison with Jane? What does this tell us about him?

Scene 21) Jane's House. Exterior. Night. As Leon walks back to his car, he is watched suspiciously by Nik who is standing beside his own car.

Scene 22) John's Car. Night. Prefaced by an overhead shot of the freeway. Valerie and John drive home from work. She asks if it worries him that they no longer make love frequently. The inference is that it worries her. He maintains that he loves her and that the number of times they have intercourse doesn't change that fact. When she tries to probe further, he asks if it is 'a test'. She reiterates that she 'simply wants to know what he is thinking' and his reply is both bemused and dismissive: 'Why do women always want to know that'. She turns away, hurt. The camera again reinforces their separate agendas by moving deliberately from one to the other, rather than showing them in the same frame.

Scene 23) Zats' House. Interior. Night. Leon arrives home late and is surprised to find Sonja still up, working. She senses that something is wrong. Leon is evasive and lies that, after 'a shit of a day', he stopped and had a drink with Claudia. The question of where he has been and what he has been doing hangs uncomfortably between them. This scene is filmed from Sonja's point of view. Throughout, Leon is shot from underneath and Sonja from above to emphasise the fact that she is disempowered by her husband's lying.

Segment 5: The Collision

Scene 24) Street. Exterior. Day. Leon collides violently with another jogger as he turns the corner. He loses his temper and abuses the man, who has broken his nose and is clearly distressed. As the man limps off, Leon runs after him to return his bag. He apologises and the man breaks down completely and sobs in Leon's arms.

Q What does Leon's behaviour reveal about his emotional state?

Scene 25a) Zats' House. Interior. Day. When Leon returns to the house, Sonja is shocked at the blood that covers his face and shirt. He tells her he fell and belligerently rejects her offer of assistance. As he washes his hands in the bathroom, he looks hard at himself in the mirror.

Scene 25b) Zats' House. Interior. Day. Sonja stands by herself in front of the window. We cannot see her face, but her body language reveals her misery. Note the mise en scène; Sonja is locked in by the windows, separated from her husband and the external world.

Key Scene

Scene 26) Valerie's Consulting Rooms. Interior. Day. Patrick accuses his lover's wife of being both 'needy' and 'manipulative': he evidently has no sympathy for the position she is in. Nor does he appear to feel any guilt for his involvement with a married man. He insists that far from being a victim, the wife has made a deliberate choice to deceive herself. When Valerie suggests that she may love her husband, Patrick counters, 'So do I'. He admits that, for him, love is 'a contest'.

Patrick's antipathy towards his lover's wife may be simply jealousy, a rationalisation, or it may be indicative of a more deep-seated misogyny. In any case, Valerie finds him somewhat threatening. While she works hard to maintain an impassive professional front, their dialogue is strained and transcends the personalities under discussion. The issue of trust is again raised. Valerie's argument that no marriage can be based on deceit and Patrick's cynical assertion that, in fact, most marriages are based on exactly that reminds us of Leon and Sonja's relationship. Does it also apply to Valerie's own circumstances? Her discomfort is compounded when Patrick provocatively contends that 'some women like to live the lie – it's easier than dealing with the truth'. He refuses to see his situation in anything except 'black and white' terms.

Q How much truth is there in Patrick's appraisal of marriage? What might it suggest about the relationships he has experienced?

Q How much sympathy do we feel for Patrick at this point? Does he know that he is intimidating Valerie? Does he care?

Scene 27) Police Station. Interior. Day. Leon thanks Claudia for covering for him the previous night. She is angry and resents being put in a compromising position: it is clear that she values Sonja's friendship. 'You don't know how lucky you are to have the marriage you've got and you're pissing all over it.'

Scene 28a) Dance Studio. Exterior. Night. Leon arrives at the dance studio, obviously late, and hurries down the stairs.

Scene 28b) Dance Studio. Interior. Night. When Leon enters, he discovers to his consternation that Sonja and Jane are dancing together. He is given another partner, but watches the two women anxiously: the proximity of his wife and lover is far too close for comfort. After their dance is finished, Sonja introduces Jane to her husband. The instructor announces that a salsa band is playing at one of the clubs and Sonja indicates she would like to go, with or without Leon. Increasingly, she is prepared to assert her independence. When the group leaves, Leon confronts Jane who assures him that she would 'never say anything'.

Segment 6: I Hate This

Scene 29) Jane's House. Interior. Night. Pete walks up the driveway to the house and lets himself in. He looks around, goes into the bedroom and picks up Jane's earrings that lie on her dressing table. The close-up of the pearls, a gift which she has admitted retains sentimental value, is an unhappy reminder of what he has lost. He leaves, disheartened.

Scene 30) Jane's House. Exterior. Night. On his way back to the car, Pete encounters Nik. He asks how his wife has been and if Nik knows of her whereabouts. He is clearly disappointed at missing her. Pete admits that he hates the situation in which he finds himself. He appeals to Nik's sense of mateship and stresses that he would want to know if Jane was 'seeing someone else'.

Key Scene

Scene 31) Bar. Interior. Night. Leon and Jane share a drink. Leon is curious as to why she and her husband have separated. When she explains that she was not prepared to live with someone whom she no longer loved, he applauds her courage and initiative. Jane acknowledges that she likes Leon 'maybe a little too much'. She is completely thrown when he confesses he is still in love with his wife and has difficulty reconciling this admission with his willingness to spend time with Jane. Leon leaves her, sitting alone in the bar. The close-ups in this scene establish a veneer of intimacy that is brutally foiled by Leon's frankness. The play of emotions on Jane's face – anticipation, followed by hurt bewilderment – is met by the rueful stoicism of Leon's expression. The scene enunciates Leon's confusion: 'I don't know – it's not something that I planned'.

Q What do you think Jane is looking for?

Q In the light of his statement 'Most people settle for less', how do you think Leon sees his own marriage?

Q What does his choice to be unfaithful show about him?

Scene 32) Restaurant. Interior. Night. Over dinner, John notes Valerie's preoccupation. She tells him of the difficulties she is experiencing with her client Patrick. John urges her to refer him on to another therapist. Abruptly, she leaves the restaurant. John watches her through the window as she crosses the street to a bookshop opposite.

Scene 33) Street. Exterior. Night. Valerie stands in front of a large promotional display advertising her book. Consider the way in which she is shot from behind, silhouetted in front of multiple copies of Eleanor's photograph. The image evokes a quasi-religious setting that commemorates and elevates her daughter's memory. At the same time, the contrast between the brightly lit display, behind the glass and therefore out of reach, and Valerie's figure, which is in deep shadow, highlights her alienation. As John comes up behind her, Valerie expresses her distress at the rift that has developed between them. She rejects his explanation ('We lost our daughter') and insists that Eleanor's death could have brought them closer together. When she asks if he thinks of their child often, he replies with contained rage, 'Of course I do. I just don't need to write a book about it'. The accusation implicit in his tone is the first intimation that he does not support the publication. As they talk, images of their murdered daughter look back at them, mute. John embraces his wife. Note, once again, the way in which close-ups are employed in this scene.

Q How realistic is Valerie being? Does this kind of tragedy bring people closer together? Can relationships recover from the grief generated by the death of a child?

Scene 34) Knoxs' Bedroom. Interior. Night. John and Valerie are making love. She is desperate that he looks at her and wants to see his face. For her, this is a greater statement of intimacy than the act of intercourse itself. Extreme close-ups are used to highlight the emotional tension between them. The final shot focuses on Valerie's expression of sorrow and resignation.

The marriage of Valerie and John appears to be dominated by grief. By their own admission, the death of their daughter has driven an unhappy wedge between them. It is a source of mutual frustration that each has reacted differently and seems unable to meet the other's needs or expectations. She has attempted to exorcise her anguish by writing a book: he has withdrawn and internalised the pain.

Segment 7: Hey Nik – Want a Coffee?

Scene 35) Nik and Paula's House. Exterior. Morning. Nik and Paula's two young children play in the lantana bush opposite their house. They join their mother who is loading up the car. Nik is holding the baby. He waves his family off and Jane, who has been watching them closely as she collects the paper, invites him over.

Scene 36) Jane's Kitchen. Interior. Morning. As they share a coffee, Nik informs Jane that Pete had been over the previous night. She refuses to be drawn into any discussion about her husband's plight and instead inquires about Nik's job hunting. She offers to help out financially 'Are you sure there isn't a bill or something?' Nik insists that they are 'fine'.

Scene 37) Knoxs' House. Interior. Morning. Prefaced by a long shot of the harbour. Valerie wakes to an empty bed. She hurries downstairs to join her husband, but he is already leaving for work. She asks him to wait for her but he is short-tempered and dismissive. She tells him she will be late home that evening. Note the way in which John shuns his wife's company after their lovemaking and the harsh contrast this presents to the intimacy of the previous night (symbolised by the unforgiving sunlight which streams across the bed when Valerie wakes). Far from bringing them closer, even temporarily, he bitterly resents being compromised by her need.

Segment 8: I Like Being This Age

KEY SCENE

Scene 38) Valerie's Consulting Rooms. Interior. Day. Sonja confides her fears to Valerie that Leon may be having an affair. She believes that she would leave the marriage if that were the case. While the prospect of life on her own is confronting and the welfare of her two sons is an important consideration, she is confident enough within herself to consider the option. She admits that the most destructive aspect of such a scenario would be the deception. 'It's not that he might have slept with another woman. It's that he might not tell me. That would be the betrayal.' When Valerie asks if Sonja still loves her husband, the question is intentionally left hanging.

Sonja's strong sense of self and refusal to compromise contrasts with Valerie's dependence. Crisis will make her stronger and more independent, whereas in Valerie's case it has exacerbated her need and her emotional reliance on her husband. Despite Sonja's misgivings, she can envisage a life of her own; Valerie is incapable of making this kind of choice. The editing and the voice-over connecting these two scenes subliminally link the respective situations of these two women. As Valerie is left wondering why John is so quick to reject her company and why he is particularly interested in the fact that she is working late, we hear Sonja's voice expressing her own fear and doubt with regard to Leon's fidelity.

Scene 39) John's Car. Day. John sits in his car, which is parked in an inner suburban laneway. He is lost in thought and ignores the phone when it rings. Note the overhead shot of the car and the way in which the camera deliberately moves down to its roof, suggesting an omniscient authority determining the fate of the occupant.

Scene 40) Valerie's Consulting Rooms. Interior. Day. The receptionist announces Patrick Phelan's arrival. Valerie asks to be given a moment – clearly she is not looking forward to his appointment.

Segment 9: An Empty Well

Scene 41) Valerie's Consulting Rooms. Interior. Day. The session commences with Patrick provocatively accusing Valerie of not liking him.

Patrick again justifies his involvement with his married lover and presents himself as a 'respite' who offers 'sex unencumbered by need' – a comment that has an uncomfortable resonance for Valerie. Valerie sees her own marriage to John exposed by Patrick's criticisms: 'Making love to her is like trying to fill an empty well'. She finds the consultation profoundly unsettling and by the time it is over her distress is palpable.

Q Note the use of camera angles in this scene. What do they communicate?

Scene 42) Valerie's Consulting Rooms. Interior. Evening. Valerie goes into the bathroom, visibly shaken by her session with Patrick. The use of cymbals conveys her sense of menace.

Scene 43) Street. Exterior. Night. Distressed and preoccupied, Valerie walks through the evening crowds. She passes Pete who is coming from the opposite direction and angrily accuses him of accosting her. She grabs his arm and screams at him, demanding to know his name.

Segment 10: Want Another Drink?

Scene 44) Hotel. Interior. Night. Leon is sitting at the bar when a shaken Pete enters and orders a double bourbon. He explains the altercation in the street with Valerie and Leon offers to buy him another drink.

Scene 45) Nik and Paula's Bedroom. Interior. Night. Prefaced by a panning shot of the car and the exterior of the house. Nik is getting ready to go out for the evening and Paula, who is folding socks on the bed, advises him to avoid the booze bus on the freeway. Nik tells his wife of Jane's invitation over that morning and jokes that their neighbour fancies him. Paula notes perceptively: 'She's lonely – and you're bored. That's a lethal combination'.

Key Scene

Scene 46) Hotel. Interior. Night. Leon and Pete stand side by side at the urinal. Leon is recounting the story of his confrontation with the distraught jogger. He concedes that the incident was his fault, but asserts, 'I don't know what makes a man cry like that'. Leon's contempt for the man is revealing: 'You fucking weak prick – pull yourself together – the rest of us have to'. When Pete suggests that men, in fact, do want to cry sometimes, Leon counters, 'Well, yeah, but you don't, do you'. Men under stress are not supposed to show their emotions; to do so violates the macho code. The empathy between Leon and Pete is immediate. They are united by mutual incomprehension of a demanding world whose expectations confound them.

Q What does this scene demonstrate about Australian men in particular?

Q How might the urinal be construed as a potent symbol of male bonding? Are there any other aspects of this scene that are culturally driven?

Scene 47) Zats' House. Interior. Night. Prefaced by long shot of the suburban skyline. Leon arrives home to find Sonja out dancing and the two boys alone. He smells cannabis and storms up the stairs to his elder son's room, bursting into it in a way that replicates the earlier drug bust. He discovers Sam smoking dope and furiously confiscates his stash.

Scene 48) Road. Night. Valerie is driving home, late at night. The camera moves between close-ups of her face and the dark expanse of road in front of her that is lit only by intermittent street lighting. The scene merges into black, followed by a tracking shot of the car from behind. The effect is predatory and evokes the menace of the scene at the very beginning of the film. The scene fades into black for a second time. Valerie is trying hard to sustain concentration. She dozes off momentarily and the car swerves violently to the other side of the road and crashes into a pole. Her mobile will not pick up a signal, so she has no alternative but to leave her vehicle and start walking.

Scene 49) Salsa Club. Interior. Night. Sonja is dancing at the salsa club with a young man who 'would like to fuck with her'. When she sees Leon arrive, she excuses herself and joins her husband at the bar. He confronts her with the fact that their son is smoking pot and she retaliates by disclosing that it was she who gave Sam permission to use the drug at home. Note the irony of his assertion that he 'won't have drugs in the house' as he puffs cigarette smoke into her face. His intolerance towards substance abuse obviously does not extend itself to nicotine. It is evident that Leon is out of touch with both his son and the needs of his wife. His inference that she is making a fool of herself at the salsa club motivates her to leave with the young man, Jose.

Scene 50) Car Park. Interior. Night. Sonja is kissing Jose in his car.

She suggests they go back to his place, but apparently 'the mother' is a problem. Sonja changes her mind; suddenly having spontaneous sex in a car with a young stranger does not seem a good idea. The boy is angry with her and drives off in disgust, leaving her alone in the car park. She limps away.

Segment 11: Pie in the Sky

Scene 51) Service Station. Exterior. Night. After walking some distance along the road, Valerie comes upon a deserted service station, aptly titled 'Pie in the Sky' (a forlorn hope). She rings her husband from the nearby phone booth, but has to leave a message on the answering machine. This scene is intercut with:

Knoxs' House. Interior. Night. The machine records Valerie's message. Again, the mise en scène of the family photographs on the table is significant – an allusion to happier times. This reverts to:

Service Station. Exterior. Night. Valerie calls John again. She has been warned of a long wait with regard to roadside assistance and becomes agitated at his continuing unresponsiveness. She leaves a second message on their machine (another cut). The third time she rings, she breaks down. She then sees a car approach and leaves the booth to flag it down.

The framing of Valerie in the phone box emphasises her isolation and vulnerability. Both literally and emotionally, she is 'walled in'. Moreover, the narrow, confined space and her increasingly despairing tone are suggestive of a confessional. She does not receive the absolution she craves, however. As she talks to John for the final time, the insinuation that he may be having an affair with her gay client hangs in the air. The approaching car conveys a feeling of impending dread, rather than rescue. This is reinforced by the blackouts on the screen, punctuating her phone calls, and the music.

Scene 52) Jane's House. Interior. Night. Jane is lying in bed when she hears Nik's truck pull up. She watches from her window as he gets out of the car, looks around furtively and throws something into the lantana bush opposite.

Scene 53) Road. Exterior. Morning. Prefaced by a long shot of bushland. Leon joins a police search, which is under way for Valerie. John has reported her missing after she did not return home the night before. Leon has a cynical bet with Claudia: 'Fifty bucks says it's the husband'.

Segment 12: What Can You Imagine?

Scene 54) Knoxs' House. Interior. Morning. Leon and Claudia interview John. They tell him Valerie's car has been located, and Leon questions John regarding his own movements and his wife's 'emotional state'. As they talk, Claudia notices Eleanor's framed photograph on the table. John maintains that he got home around midnight the previous evening. He gives the police a photo of Valerie and, with greater reluctance, the tape from the answering machine.

Scene 55) Nik and Paula's House. Interior. Morning. Paula is getting ready for work. She hands the baby to Nik, who is still in bed, to feed. She observes the scratches on his face and he tells her that he fell over. He seems preoccupied. As the camera pans slowly towards Nik, the accompanying music suggests something amiss.

Scene 56) Nik and Paula's House. Exterior. Morning. As Paula is about to drive off, Jane jogs up to the car. She comments that Nik got in late the night before. Paula responds tersely and asks her not to have Nik in for coffee in her absence.

Scene 57) Valerie's Consulting Rooms. Interior. Day. Leon asks Valerie's receptionist for a list of her clients, though he admits this is not entirely ethical. He removes the tape of Patrick Phelan's last session from Valerie's dictaphone. As he searches through her files, he discovers that his own wife is a client. He takes Sonja's tape.

Scene 58a) Jane's House. Interior. Day. Jane watches Nik closely from her window as he leaves with the baby in the pusher.

Scene 58b) Vacant Block. Exterior. Day. Jane walks towards the lantana bush, curious to find what Nik threw away the previous night. Both the camera work (slowly moving into a close-up of the bush so that it ultimately fills the screen) and the music connect this scene with the opening sequence and generate an uneasy sense of *deja vu*. What secret does the lantana hide? When Nik turns back unexpectedly, Jane ducks into the bush. She finds a woman's shoe and hides quietly herself while Nik checks if anything can be seen from the street. The close-up of her face, as she crouches out of sight, registers her trepidation.

Scene 59) Leon's Car. Day. Leon listens to the tape recording of Sonja's last consultation with Valerie. When she is asked if she still loves her husband, Leon stops the tape. He cannot bear to hear the answer.

Scene 60) Zats' Living Room. Interior. Night. Valerie's disappearance is reported on the evening news. As Sonja and her younger son watch the television, this scene is intercut with Nik and Paula, then Jane, each watching the same ABC report. As the scanty details of Valerie's accident are relayed, reference is also made to Eleanor Knox's fate, two years earlier.

Segment 13: You're a Prick!

Scene 61a) Leon's Car. Night. Leon drives John through the tunnel as they retrace Valerie's final journey. They arrive at the phone booth where the police have set up a life-size mannequin simulating Valerie's hailing of the car.

Scene 61b) Roadside. Exterior. Night. Leon tries to elicit further information from John. He asks about the route Valerie took on the night she disappeared and her relationship with Patrick Phelan. He also asks John to clarify his own movements on the Friday night in question. It is clear that Leon is suspicious of Valerie's husband and he implies that John knows more than he is admitting. The hostility between the two men is undisguised. Note Leon's virtuous assertion that he tells his wife 'everything' and John's cynical and accurate rebuttal. 'That surprises me – most men hold something back.'

The film has now switched focus so that the mystery alluded to at the outset takes centre stage. The police enquiry instigated by Valerie's untimely disappearance dominates the narrative and Leon is called on to perform in a professional capacity as the investigating officer. By a bizarre coincidence, the missing woman has been professionally treating his own wife. It would seem that Valerie is dead – the exact circumstances, whether or not she has been murdered, remains unknown. Leon's suspicions of John are based on precedent and experience: 'nine times out of ten, when the wife goes missing, the husband knows something about it'. However, our attention has been drawn to Nik. His preoccupation the morning after Valerie's accident, the scratch on his face and, most importantly, the surreptitious throwing of the shoe into the lantana suggest guilt. Jane herself feels that she has to hide from Nik. She is suddenly suspicious of the neighbour whom she knows well and fearful of his responses.

Scene 62) Leon's Car. Night. As he drives back to the station, Leon listens to the tape recording of Patrick's last session with Valerie.

Scene 63) Police Station. Interior. Night. Claudia is reading Valerie's book, *Eleanor*, at her desk. She notes that Valerie has dedicated the book to her husband, John, 'For teaching me to trust again'. Leon tells Claudia to go home – it is late – and she advises him to do likewise. Before she leaves, Leon asks her if she has talked to the 'mystery man' yet, but she ruefully explains that he never came back. Once again, the affection between the two partners is evident.

Scene 64) Zats' Bedroom. Interior. Night. Sonja is in bed when Leon returns. She enquires about the missing woman and Leon tells her that it is not looking good. He also reveals that he saw Valerie's client list. He is disarmed by Sonja's rationale that seeking counselling was something 'private' she had to do. 'There was a time when there was no private between you and me.'

Scene 65) Zats' House. Interior. Night. Sonja joins her husband on the stairs and he confesses that he has been seeing another woman. When she asks why, he replies '...because I'm numb – I can't feel anything any more – just totally fucking numb'. Sonja is devastated, unable to respond. The camera focuses instead on her body language – the hand to her chest, the laboured breathing, her stricken expression – and the final close-up of the hurt and shock written on her face.

Q Why does Leon decide to tell the truth at this point?

The realisation that Sonja is also unhappy in their marriage jolts Leon out of his self-absorption. In admitting that his affair with Jane hurts both his wife and his lover, he is finally demonstrating an awareness of the consequences of his choices. It has been a lose-lose scenario for all concerned. Telling Sonja the truth is the first step towards reconciling their interests. It is ironic that Sonja herself feels defensive about keeping her counselling sessions with Valerie private, when Leon has been hiding something far more serious from her. We are reminded of Valerie's contention that trust is fundamental to all worthwhile relationships including, of course, marriage.

KEY SCENE

Scene 66a) Zats' House. Interior. Morning. When Dylan, the younger son, comes down for school, he observes that Leon has slept on the couch and immediately recognises that his parents are fighting. His protective concern for his mother suggests that this kind of discord is an aberration. After the boys go out to the car Leon tries to address the issue with Sonja, but she doesn't want to have anything to do with him.

'You know what's so easy Leon – it's so easy to go out and find someone. You know what's hard – what's hard is not to.' Sonja's sense of betrayal is compounded by the fact that, despite her unhappiness, she has *not* taken the easy option. Staying in a relationship even when it is not meeting expectations, working at the day-to-day concerns, and trying to improve circumstances from the inside – keeping the faith, in other words – takes courage and commitment. Moreover, Sonja is very aware of the 'big picture' and understands full well that the marriage is not just about her and Leon. They have two sons whose welfare is a consideration and whose lives would be profoundly affected by their parents' decisions. Leon's excuse is simply that 'he fucked up'. When he asks if Sonja will continue to 'punish' him, he is oversimplifying the issues. He still has a long way to go in terms of acknowledging the full repercussions of his adultery.

Q In this scene it is apparent that the house is undergoing renovation. What does the yellow mini-skip outside on the street suggest?

Scene 66b) Zats' House. Exterior. Day. As Sonja leaves the house, she meets Claudia and asks her angrily if she knew about Leon's infidelity. Sonja correctly interprets Claudia's uncomfortable silence as a 'yes'. She drives off in disgust.

Scene 66c) Zats' House. Interior. Day. Claudia goes inside to collect her partner, who is standing unhappily in the kitchen.

Scene 67) Jane's House. Interior. Day. Jane sits contemplating Valerie's shoe, which sits on a small table in her living room. She looks out of the window at Nik who is playing with his son. Close-up of the lantana in bloom. After some deliberation, she rings Pete and asks him to come over.

Segment 14: That's My Life!

Scene 68) Apartment Block. Interior. Day. Prefaced by an overhead shot of Leon and Claudia as they drive to the block of flats where Patrick Phelan lives. Before the interview, Claudia asks Leon if he is 'up to it'. However, despite his insistence that he is fine, Leon's response to Patrick is far more aggressive than is warranted. He hectors Patrick about his last appointment with Valerie and his 'boyfriend' and manhandles him, as he demands to know who is in Patrick's bedroom. The man he does find is a stranger.

Scene 69) Lobby. Interior. Day. As they walk from the lift, Claudia tackles Leon over his attitude. Leon will not concede that he was in the wrong.

Scene: 70) Laneway. Exterior. Day. John leaves flowers by a step in the narrow lane where his daughter's body was discovered. There are several bunches of dead flowers already there.

Scene 71) Leon's Car. Day. Leon rings home, hoping to speak to Sonja. This scene is intercut with:

Zats' Kitchen. Interior. Day. Dylan answers the phone, but Sonja refuses to take the call. (Cut) Leon tells Dylan that he will be home soon. (Cut) Dylan provides his mother with his own version of Leon's message and reports that 'he said to say that he's sorry, that he loves you, and he wants you to stop being angry at him'. Sonja's loving close-up as she looks at her young son expresses her appreciation at his clumsy lie.

Key Scene

Scene 72) Knoxs' House. Exterior. Day. John arrives home to find Leon waiting for him. They sit out on the deck and share a whisky. Leon quizzes John again on his movements the night of Valerie's disappearance. He tells him that his wife thought he might be having an affair with Patrick Phelan and asks if there is any truth to this. John admits that there was someone in the past – a woman – and that once that happens 'something gets broken'. He explains that the night in question he stopped at the place that Eleanor was killed and that Valerie did not know of his regular visits to the laneway. He tries to give Leon a sense of what his marriage has been like and the way in which their daughter's death has impacted on his and Valerie's relationship.

Q Why would John keep from his wife the fact that he regularly visits the site of their daughter's murder?

Q How much do Leon and John have in common?

Despite Leon's role as investigating cop, it is John who directs the line of questioning throughout this scene. When he asks Leon if he has ever cheated on his wife, Leon's awkward denial is another lie – small in the overall scheme of things – but it may suggest that he has still not come to terms with his own conduct. John's rueful observation that 'once that's happened, you are never entirely believed again' challenges Leon to consider the long-term impact of his infidelity on his relationship with Sonja. Can trust be rebuilt? Is it possible for them to work through this crisis and what residual damage will be the legacy? John's query as to what holds Leon's marriage together prompts the response 'Loyalty, love, maybe habit, sometimes passion – our kids'. It is interesting that Leon cites loyalty first. Is he thinking of himself or Sonja? Note the framing of the two men at the end of this scene – their positions as they sit at the table and the distance between them. What might this suggest? Consider the ideas that have been raised through the course of their dialogue, as well as their respective dilemmas.

Segment 15: The Shoe

Scene 73a) Police Station. Interior. Day. When Leon arrives back at the station, Claudia informs him that they have received a report, which may be the breakthrough they need. A woman saw her neighbour throw a woman's shoe into a vacant lot the night Valerie disappeared. She has found the shoe.

Scene 73b) Leon's Car. Day. Leon and Claudia pull up in front of Jane's house. Leon explains that it could be 'tricky' as he knows her.

Scene 74) Jane's House. Interior. Day. Pete opens the door and recognises Leon immediately, which rattles him even further. Leon tells Jane she should not have touched the shoe. The awkward stalemate between them is broken by Claudia, who suggests coffee. When the others leave the room, Leon asks Jane if she is all right. She tells him bluntly to just do his job.

Scene 75) Nik and Paula's House. Interior. Day. Nik watches the police approach through the window as he tries to phone Paula. Claudia knocks on the door to take him into custody, but says she will give him a couple of minutes to organise child care for his kids. The close-ups of Hannah's face underline Nik's role as the father of a young family.

Scene 76) Jane's House. Day. Leon listens as Jane gives her statement to the constable. Meanwhile, the police comb the vacant block opposite the house. When Leon goes outside to join Claudia, he meets Nik approaching Jane's house with his three children.

Scene 77) Jane's House. Interior. Day. Nik asks Jane and Pete to mind the children until Paula's return. He explains that he's in 'a bit of trouble'. Jane is hesitant, but agrees.

Scene 78) Police Station. Interior. Day. Belligerently, Leon interrogates Nik about the scratches on his face and his whereabouts Friday night. Nik keeps repeating that he wants to see his wife. He then recognises Leon as the man whom Jane has been seeing. Once again, Claudia and Leon seem to respectively assume the 'good cop / bad cop' roles that have characterised their professional dealings to date.

Segment 16: I Don't Wanna Calm Down!

Scene 79) Police Station. Interior. Day. Paula arrives at the station, frantic to know where her children are and what is going on. Claudia ushers her into a waiting room.

Scene 80) Police Station. Interior. Night. Leon explains to Paula that Nik is 'helping them with their enquiries'. He tells Paula of the discovery of Valerie's shoe and Nik's involvement in the drama.

Scene 81) Police Station. Interior. Night. Nik is alone in the interview room. He calls out for his wife.

Scene 82a) Police Station. Interior. Night. A subdued Paula rings Jane to thank her for having the children. She asks to speak to Hannah, her eldest daughter. This scene is constantly intercut with:

Scene 82b) Jane's House. Interior. Night. Jane reassures her that the children are settled. Pete is with her. Paula is tearful and apologetic. She explains that Nik is in trouble and that she has still not been allowed to see him. When she hangs up, Pete asks Jane if Paula knows if it was she who reported her husband to the police. Jane shakes her head, upset by the conversation.

KEY SCENE

Scene 83) Police Station. Interior. Night. Paula is finally led into the room where Nik has been waiting. She anxiously confronts him with the police charge that he has hurt 'some woman'. Nik denies the accusation categorically and Paula goes over to embrace him. Leon watches them both closely, moved and unsettled.

Despite its brevity, this scene is a crucial one. It encapsulates the defining qualities that underscore Nik and Paula's marriage, making it special and, within the context, unique. The unquestioning support and trust which Paula is prepared to offer her husband contrasts with the various emotional betrayals evident in other relationships explored in the text. Nik does not have to explain or rationalise his position to his wife. Paula simply believes he is telling the truth because honesty is a fundamental criterion of their partnership. Note the way in which close-ups are employed in this scene to highlight the range of emotions – the initial confusion and defensiveness written on Paula's face, Nik's imploring expression, and finally Paula's loving acceptance of whatever role he may or may not have played in Valerie's disappearance. Leon observes this 'dialogue' with a professional scepticism that changes to humility, reminded no doubt of his own shortcomings as a husband.

Scene 84a) Jane's House. Interior. Night. As Pete and Jane lie on the bed together, Pete attempts to caress his wife, but is rebuffed. They are interrupted by Hannah, who tells them the baby is sick. He is feverish and needs some medication.

Scene 84b) Nik and Paula's House. Interior. Night. Jane goes next door to get some Baby Panadol. She cannot help but notice the untidy state of the living room.

Scene 85a) Police Station. Interior. Night. Nik tells his story to Leon and Claudia. On the night in question, he met some mates for a drink, and on his way home, took the back road to avoid the police. This scene is intercut with:

KEY SCENE

Scene 85b) Road. Night. Nik's voice-over continues the narration. A woman hails him down and tells him she has had an accident. He offers her a lift, although he would have preferred to go straight home. They introduce themselves; she is nervous and reluctant to talk. As it turns out, she lives in the opposite direction. (Cut) However, there is a short cut and, without thinking, he turns off the main road. (Cut) Valerie is so frightened at driving into the bush that she panics and jumps out of the car. Nik tries to follow her, but trips. He calls to her to stop: 'Trust me'. She hides, then runs blindly and goes into free fall. (Cut) Nik explains to his audience that he left her, assuming she would be all right. He disposed of the shoe that was left in his car and, when he subsequently saw on the news that Valerie was missing, he saw no alternative but to keep quiet.

This scene is the denouement – the point at which the mystery is exposed and we learn the truth behind Valerie's accident. While Nik is obviously implicated, his involvement in her death has been entirely inadvertent. The worst he could be accused of is trying to avoid a breathalysing test. Paula's faith in her husband is vindicated and the unlikelihood of this father of three deliberately hurting a vulnerable woman is reinforced by his plaintive defence, 'Jesus, I just wanted to help the woman'. His tearful explanation, 'I thought that if I leave her alone, she'll stop being afraid of me', strikes a chord with the listening coppers, as does his reason for not reporting the events of the fateful night. The irony of Valerie's predicament becomes clear. Her extreme wariness at accepting a lift from a stranger in the first place relates back to the tragic circumstances of Eleanor's murder, and the fragile trust she is prepared to grant Nik is completely shattered when he deviates from the main road. Her fear that he intends to harm her is such that she is incapable of trusting him any further, and it is her fear that precipitates her death. Throughout the interview, Nik is shot from above as if to emphasise the way in which he has been caught up in circumstances beyond his control.

Segment 17: He Didn't Do It

Scene 86) Knoxs' House. Interior. Morning. Long shot of day breaking over the bushland. John takes a call from Leon. He thanks him.

Scene 87) Jane's House. Day. Paula arrives home to collect her children from Jane's house. She is hostile towards her neighbour and tells her that Nik is innocent. When Jane responds sceptically, Paula retaliates with devastating simplicity that she knows it to be true because 'he told me'. She leaves with Jane's protests ringing in her ears.

Scene 88) Nik and Paula's House. Day. When Paula enters her own house, it is immaculate. Furious, she goes into her backyard and calls over the fence to Jane to stay out of her family's life. Cut to Jane's kitchen as she listens to Paula's abuse. (Cut) Paula is angry at the role Jane has played in the drama and cannot bear the thought of being in the other woman's debt. The high angle shot highlights her sense of impotence. (Fade) Jane sits on her bed, alone and brooding.

Scene 89) Bushland. Exterior. Day. Prefaced by a close-up of the lantana. Valerie's body is winched up a cliff face as Leon and Claudia supervise the police search. Nik has been helping them locate the body. Valerie's bruised hand falls out of the body bag; Leon gently puts it back and zips it up. John arrives in a police car to identify his wife's body. He confesses to Leon that he was home on the night of her disappearance, and did not pick up the phone. The scene reverts to John and Valerie's house. John is listening to the answering machine recording Valerie's message as he prepares dinner. (Cut) He tells Leon, 'I thought she would come home'.

Q Why doesn't John answer Valerie's call? Consider the guilt he now feels.

Scene 90) Leon's Car. Day. Leon returns to his own car and listens to Sonja's tape. He hears her affirm the fact that she does love him. He breaks down and cries bitterly as the enormity of what he has risked losing hits home.

Q Are you surprised to find out Sonja's answer? Why has Leon waited until now to access her response?

Scene 91a) Leon's Car. Day. Claudia drives Leon home. He gets out without a word, still overwrought.

Scene 91b) Zats' House. Exterior. Day. Leon goes through to the garden where Sonja sits by herself. She looks at him, emotionally exhausted. He tells her that he doesn't want to lose her. 'I couldn't bear it.' His grief and guilt are matched by her heartbroken ambivalence. Close-ups reinforce the emotional intensity of the moment.

Epilogue

The final montage economically draws together the key threads of the drama and the respective fates of the players are resolved. Accompanied by the whimsical rhythm of a Latin melody, we see the following scenes:

- Leon lies on the bed, miserable and uncertain of what the future holds.
- Jane dances by herself in her living room, swaying as she gives herself up to the music.
- A dejected Pete drives away from their house.
- Claudia is having dinner in the restaurant. She watches her mystery man enter and sit down. He then comes over to her table and, to her delight, joins her. 'Mystery man' turns out to be the jogger with whom Leon collided.
- Patrick forlornly watches his lover through a restaurant window as the man happily shares a meal with his wife and son.
- Nik, Paula and their three children relax in their garden, the picture of contented domesticity.
- John stands alone, looking out over the ocean.
- Sonja goes into the bedroom and lies down with her husband. Leon draws her close to him.
- Leon and Sonja dance slowly together. He looks at her with great passion; she returns his gaze. They are totally focused on each other.

CHARACTERS & RELATIONSHIPS

Lantana is essentially an ensemble piece, which explores the interaction between a number of individuals, many of whom are in relationships of one sort or another. The character of Leon is the central pivot, around which the other characters revolve. Andrew Bovell has termed Leon's journey as the 'spine of the film'.[8]

---

[8] Bovell, *Lantana* Screenplay, p.10.

Leon

Key Quotes

'Why are you trying so hard to fuck up your life?' (Sc.27, Claudia)
'I don't want to die.' (Sc.6)
'This is not an affair. It's a one night stand, except it happened twice.' (Sc.20)
'I'm still in love with my wife.' (Sc.31)
'I'm a cop.' (Sc.47)
'You're a prick.' (Sc.61b, John)
'Don't you have a home to go to?' (Sc.63, Claudia)
'Your marriage is falling apart and so are you.' (Sc.69, Claudia)
'You haven't been around much lately.' (Sc.49, Sonja)
'I'm numb – I can't feel anything any more.' (Sc.65)
'I don't want to lose you. I couldn't bear it.' (Sc.91b)

Detective Sergeant Leon Zat is a mass of contradictions. He loves his wife, but is playing around with Jane. He values his family, yet his actions jeopardise its wellbeing. While he is a concerned parent, he has little appreciation of what is going on in his sons' lives. He is capable of behaving violently, but is also both humorous and affectionate. He is anxious enough for his health to stubbornly maintain a fitness program that affords him no joy, but, at the same time, he smokes. Played brilliantly by Anthony LaPaglia, Leon is a complex, dour, at times alienating, but ultimately sympathetic individual.

When the film opens, he appears to be at a crossroad. He feels stale and dissatisfied with himself. According to his partner and friend, Claudia, he is wilfully sabotaging his life, 'pissing over' (Sc.27) his marriage. He has fallen into a relationship with Jane as a response to the ennui that can accompany even the best of marriages after a long period of time. His role in this affair is essentially reactive: 'It's not something that I planned' (Sc.31). He is unable to articulate just what it is that has gone wrong in his relationship with his wife, except to say he's 'fucking numb' (Sc.65). However, Jane's assumption that they *are* having an affair is a turning point. It formalises something that, in Leon's mind, is casual and random, and the implications are unacceptable. He is unable to lie to himself or to Sonja long-term. Moreover, he is unnerved when the different elements of his life intersect, and the professional collides with the clandestine. The last thing he expects is for his wife to have an association with the woman whose disappearance he is investigating, or for his lover to provide evidence against a suspect. Or even to meet his lover's husband in a bar. These unwelcome coincidences act as a catalyst, which forces him to reappraise his behaviour and allows his essential integrity to reassert itself.

Equally, some of the people he encounters in the course of this investigation act as a trigger and his interaction with them invites reflection. His relationship with John Knox is interesting. The two men, on the face of it, have little in common. The sneering anti-intellectualism Leon initially displays – 'you're some kind of academic' (Sc.61b) – highlights their differences. Ironically, it is John who recognises Leon's vulnerability – 'you look bereft' (Sc.72) – which leads to an exchange of confidences about their respective marriages and provides Leon with an opportunity to react honestly. He is both challenged and cautioned by John's predicament. The mutual antagonism that has characterised the relationship is defused and evolves into a grudging complicity. By the time John confesses that he was actually home on the night of Valerie's death, Leon is unwilling to be judgmental and instead feels genuine sympathy for the other man.

Being a policeman is an important part of Leon's persona. Professionally, he is a pragmatist; for example, he is prepared to access Valerie's confidential files if it will help, despite the questionable ethics of such a strategy. He is an aggressive interrogator who often uses intimidation as a tool. His partnership with Claudia oscillates between a 'big brother' and an almost paternalistic role. It is in the context of this relationship that we see his capacity for humour. His gentle ribbings about her 'mystery man' underline his very real affection for her and his concern for her welfare. The fact that Leon is a cop infiltrates his relationship with his sons. When he catches Sam smoking dope, he cannot help but fall into character and has a rather simplistic reaction to the issue.

Like many men, Leon internalises his confusion and emotional pain. His emotional defences are well contained and his episodic violence provides the only (unhealthy) outlet. He demonstrates a macho intolerance for any kind of perceived weakness; for example, his response to the man whose nose he breaks is brutal and unforgiving. Men have been conditioned to believe that they should never cry, regardless of whatever kind of crisis is going on in their lives. Paradoxically, Leon is frustrated by his eldest son's lack of demonstrativeness: 'Is there some point where a son stops kissing his father?' (Sc.6). Of course, when Leon breaks down and sobs uncontrollably at the end of the film, he is a stronger man for it. Expressing pain and acknowledging need is a necessary step on the journey to emotional maturity. He is dependent on Sonja in a way that he is barely able to allow and the possibility of losing her overwhelms him. Leon moves from being 'numb' to demonstrating a humble recognition of the value of his marriage and family. The passion and intensity that charge the final scene as Leon and Sonja dance together suggests that this marriage has weathered the crisis, and the pair's commitment to each other is mutual and inviolable.

Sonja

Key Quotes

'I want more – I want more than that.' (Sc.10)
'Passionate and challenging and [emotionally] honest.' (Sc.10, Sonja's response to Valerie's question regarding her expectations of marriage.)
'I like being this age, and I like the lines around my eyes…' (Sc.38)
'I would survive if I had to.' (Sc.38)
'You know what's so easy Leon – it's so easy to go out and find somebody. You know what's hard – what's hard is not to.' (Sc.66a)

Sonja is the linchpin that holds the Zat family together. She is a supportive wife and a loving mother who enjoys a close relationship with both her sons. Their welfare is a clear priority and when she talks through the issue of her marriage with Valerie her concern for them is evident. While she adores them both, she does not baby them; for example, the insouciant shrug she offers Sam suggests that his lack of a clean school uniform is his problem. She is in touch with her sons' needs and is a tolerant, lateral-thinking parent. She is prepared to condone Sam, her sixteen-year-old, smoking cannabis in the house on the basis that at least she knows where he is and what he is doing. This contrasts with the heavy-handed way in which Leon addresses the issue. In turn, the protective support that the boys show towards Sonja when their parents' dissension becomes apparent to them is touching.

Our first view of Sonja, as she waits for her husband, is a radiant close-up. As she turns to greet Leon, we receive the impression of a warm, confident personality. While she is not happy, Sonja has enough faith in her marriage to proactively seek advice and enough commitment to try to work through the issues that trouble her. Her sessions with Valerie highlight her resilience and strong sense of self: 'I like the lines around my eyes. I don't know if he does but I do…' (Sc.38). She finds Leon's admission of adultery utterly demoralising, given that she has not allowed herself the same option. Her choice not to have sex with the boy from the salsa club is partly based on an adult distaste for casual fornication in the back seat of a car. It is also a clear rejection of an action that could undermine her marriage even further. In this context, Leon's betrayal seems to mock the loyalty she has shown.

The fact that Sonja still forgives Leon for his infidelity is a testimony to her generosity and love. The anguished uncertainty revealed on her face as she turns to confront her husband in the final scene shows clearly that this is a no-win situation for her. There is little consolation in the fact that she is in the right and he is unequivocally in the wrong. Nevertheless, Sonja has the courage to make the first move towards reconciling their differences. The marital bed becomes the symbol of healing and the concluding image of Leon and Sonja dancing as a couple reminds us of the journey these two have travelled. The divisive dance class of the past, where Leon's reluctance and conservatism have clashed with Sonja's liberal-mindedness and sense of adventure, is now a powerful expression of their intimacy.

Claudia

Key Quotes

'Not with the hours I keep.' (Sc.9)
'I'll lie for you to anyone except Sonja. I've done it once – I won't do it again.' (Sc.27)
'There is someone…He eats in the same restaurant as I do.' (Sc.9)

Claudia Weis is Leon's partner and the close proximity of their working relationship means that she understands him well. As a team, she and Leon complement each other; her sympathetic persona balances the more abrasive tactics he often employs. Claudia does not always approve of what she observes and does not hesitate to tell her colleague so, almost acting as the voice of his conscience on occasion. She is critical with regard to some aspects of Leon's professional modus operandi; for example, the unwarranted violence he demonstrates during the drug bust and the unacceptable manner in which he harasses Patrick Phelan during his 'interview'. She, quite rightly, perceives that Leon's belligerence has more to do with the implosion of his personal life than anything in their job description. She is on solid ground when she asserts, 'It *is* my business if you can't do your job' (Sc.69).

Claudia is equally blunt with regard to the marital hole Leon is digging for himself. She is perceptive enough to suspect something is brewing when Leon first introduces her to Jane, and although she subsequently covers for him she makes it clear that it's a one-off. 'I'll lie for you to anyone except Sonja' (Sc.27). She admires Sonja and resents being drawn into the deception. Not only is it an affront to her own integrity, she is also intolerant of the fact that Leon is jeopardising the very fundamentals she herself aspires to: family and a loving partner. Nevertheless, despite her disapproval, her loyalties are with Leon whom she regards as a mentor and a friend. It is precisely because of her fondness for him that she finds it hard to stand aside and watch him 'fuck up his life' (Sc.27). When Sonja does discover her husband's infidelity, Claudia is made to feel, rather unfairly, guilty by association.

As a young, female cop working in a male-dominated workplace, Claudia has had to develop strategies to survive. A sense of humour and an ability to 'give and take' stand her in good stead. The workload is such that opportunities for a social life outside the force are limited. Her hours are irregular and she eats by herself in restaurants, rather than cook. By her own admission, she is rather lonely and would relish the opportunity to meet someone. Claudia is an engaging, honest and generous woman with much to offer, and one of the more feelgood aspects of the film's ending is the suggestion that she and her 'mystery man' will finally get together. The fact that he turns out to be 'the weak prick' (Sc.46) with whom Leon collided is just another of the unexpected coincidences on which the film is predicated. What Leon will make of this discovery remains to be seen!

Jane

Key Quotes

'You're a brave woman. You are. Most people settle for less.' (Sc.31, Leon)
'You just have this kind of look – full of potential.' (Sc.28b, Sonja)
'Maybe my expectations were too high.' (Sc.31)
'She's lonely, Nik.' (Sc.45, Paula)

As the 'other woman' and a deliberate foil to Sonja, Jane does not invite our sympathy to the same degree. However, Paula's summation is accurate; Jane *is* lonely and, by extension, vulnerable. She is deliberately looking for new romantic options and joining a dance class may be one way to meet people. She ironically makes reference to her 'desperate' single status as she is dancing with Sonja: 'Can you tell?' (Sc.28b). It is Jane who takes the predatory role in the relationship with Leon; she waits for him outside the station and is forthright about her attraction for him. When he makes it clear that he is not interested in pursuing the affair, she is initially hurt and then angry. Her resentment is apparent when Leon arrives to interview her over the discovery of Valerie's shoe.

Whether Jane has 'high expectations' or whether the break-up of her marriage simply highlights an inability to sustain a relationship through the tough times is unclear. It is evident that she envies Nik and Paula's relationship; her wistful expression as she watches the affection they display towards each other is revealing. She clearly finds Nik appealing and though his assumption that she is actively 'coming on to him' (Sc.45) is probably an overstatement, from Paula's perspective, Jane becomes something of a threat. The relationship between the two women, initially close, breaks down utterly after Nik's apprehension by the police, with Paula abusing Jane over the back fence. Jane has obviously deliberated over whether or not she should implicate Nik in the investigation and is hurt by the inevitable estrangement that follows.

Like many of the other characters in *Lantana*, Jane is driven by disappointment. Her marriage has not proved satisfactory, nor is her single status offering the opportunities she had hoped for. Despite her free-spirited persona and her desire for independence, Jane reverts to needing Pete's support when confronted with an emergency. Interestingly, she continues to wear her wedding ring, maintaining that it is too tight to remove and will have to be cut off. She selfishly does not consider the emotional impact on Pete when she calls for his help and has no hesitation about sending him on his way once the immediate crisis is over. Throughout the text, Jane is represented as a voyeur, someone who lives vicariously through her neighbours, feeding off their daily dramas. We often see her, filmed in subdued lighting, looking out the window at the comings and goings of the house next door. Aside from the affair with Leon, we see little evidence of a life outside her home. Paula at one point says to her in frustration, 'Haven't you got anything better to do than spy on your neighbours?' (Sc.56). The simple answer would appear to be no. There is considerable irony in Sonja's observation that Jane is 'full of potential' (Sc.28b). Contrast this with the final image of her dancing by herself, again, cigarette in one hand and drink in the other.

Pete

Key Quotes

'I hate this.' (Sc.30)
'But don't you want to cry sometimes?' (Sc.46)

Pete O'May is a genial, uncomplicated man who is out of his depth. His wife has left him and he is miserable. He struggles to articulate his feelings and is reduced to simple, but heartfelt expressions of angst that only hint at his despair. The marital break is not of his choosing and he, rather forlornly, hopes for a reconciliation, unwilling or unable to move on. He visits Jane's house, desperate for a glimpse of his wife. He tries to keep track of her movements through Nik. Pete is supportive of his former spouse; she only has to pick up the phone and ask for his help and he is on her doorstep. He is eager to be of use when Jane is asked to mind their neighbours' children for the night and sees it as an opportunity to further his cause with her. Note the way in which he tentatively reaches out to her when he stays the night. Pete is essentially a 'man's man', more comfortable in the company of other men and confused by the perplexing requirements of the female psyche. The pub, with its familiar and reassuring landscape, is the obvious retreat after the disconcerting experience of being targeted by Valerie in the street. Pete is a sad and lonely figure as he drives away from his former home, presumably for the last time.

Valerie

Key Quotes

'Can we believe in love? Feel safe in it?' (Sc.12)
'Two years ago, my eleven-year-old daughter was murdered.' (Sc.12)
'I hate what's happening to us.' (Sc.33)
'She was afraid (of being alone). Of me not being there for her.' (Sc.72, John)

Dr Valerie Somers is a psychiatrist. On the surface, she is a skilled and successful practitioner, used to exercising control in her professional life. Indeed, her capacity to help others is one of the ways in which she is able to maintain her equilibrium. In this role, she projects an assured facade and at the book launch she acts as a spokesperson for her audience, raising questions and articulating general concerns in an authoritative, yet empathetic manner. Conversely, her personal life reveals a fragility and insecurity that threatens to completely overwhelm her on occasion. The defining experience in Valerie's life has been the brutal murder of her young daughter, Eleanor. The devastation that both she and John feel is such that there seems no way to work through, or around, the event; the fallout is inescapable. It has distorted their relationship, placing enormous pressure on them as a couple, and they are polarised by their misery. Valerie has assumed ownership over the grieving process. The fact that she has written and published a book, and is subsequently involved in its promotion, makes her the public face of the tragedy: 'I just wanted the world to know' (Sc.33). At the book launch, she talks of 'my' rather than 'our' daughter; John is merely the supportive spouse in the crowd. Once home, she maintains her nightly ritual of lighting candles in Eleanor's bedroom, their daughter's memory officially perpetuated through her actions.

When Valerie asks her audience if it is possible to believe in love, feel safe in it, the question goes to the heart of her dilemma. She no longer feels safe, emotionally or physically. While her husband contains his emotions and is prepared to rationalise the rift between them, 'You don't lose a daughter like we lost Eleanor without some damage' (Sc.72), Valerie rages against the ensuing loss of intimacy within the marriage. As a therapist, she uses language to communicate feelings, to expose the truth. She needs to talk, to share ideas, to work through issues. The silences with John resonate with unresolved questions that, for her, are a further source of pain and frustration. The more she tries to force intimacy with him, the more he withdraws. When they make love, she insists that he look at her. For her, this represents a connection that is not necessarily implied by the act of intercourse itself. However, he feels overwhelmed by her need and ultimately resists it.

Valerie is not so lacking in personal insight that she is unaware of her own predicament. She relates uneasily to Patrick's evaluation of his lover's wife as 'very needy' (Sc.26). A part of her recognises herself in his description and senses that this might be the way in which her own husband views her. However, the fact that she perceives Patrick's comments to be personally directed highlights her emotional vulnerability. Although she credits John with teaching her 'to trust again' (Sc.63) after their daughter's murder, the legacy of Eleanor's death has left Valerie unable to differentiate between what is 'trustworthy' and what is not. She misinterprets Patrick's criticism and jumps to the erroneous conclusion that he may be having an affair with her own husband: Her paranoia subsequently leads her to target the inoffensive Pete as a threat. Nevertheless, Valerie's fear of being alone is even greater than her fear of danger. Consequently, she gets into a car with a stranger. It is a bitter irony that she is not able to trust Nik, whose motives are entirely honourable and whose only intention is to help her.

John

Key Quotes

'You don't lose a daughter like we lost Eleanor without some damage.' (Sc.72)
'Ours (their marriage) is held together by grief.' (Sc.72)
I'm saying that sometimes love isn't enough.' (Sc.72)
'Don't be deceived by appearances.' (Sc.72)
'I stopped at the place where my daughter was killed. I go there a lot.' (Sc.72)

John Knox is a Professor of Law, a professional academic. He studied at Harvard University and it was here that he and Valerie met. He is a private and reserved man whose response to Eleanor's death is diametrically at odds with his wife's. They grieve in different ways. The private communion with his daughter's memory, visiting the site of her murder, leaving flowers, is something he is unwilling or unable to share with Valerie. There is the suggestion that he finds the publication of her book gratuitous, even distasteful. He is resigned to their life together, with its attendant heartache; he intellectualises their situation and demonstrates dogged loyalty with regard to the marriage. He may disapprove of Valerie's book, but he is a supportive presence at the launch, there because 'I said I would be' (Sc.13).

However, John resents Valerie's emotional dependence and resists intimacy with her. He has withdrawn physically and, when she tries to draw him out, he closes down, suspicious of her motives: 'Is this a test'

(Sc.22). Note the subtle way in which he patronises her when he generalises regarding women's desire to know what their partners are thinking. Also note the intolerance he shows towards her when he feels she is not giving him sufficient space. It becomes clear that his responses to his wife are a defensive strategy. His own pain is such that he simply does not possess the resources to fulfil her emotional demands as well. Notwithstanding the intolerable pressure that Eleanor's murder has placed on them both, it may be that Valerie's need for reassurance, for overt commitment, has always been problematic. John *did* have an affair in the past and has had to fight the legacy of mistrust ever since: 'Once that's happened, you're never entirely believed again' (Sc.72).

John is not always a sympathetic character – he can be prickly and his natural reserve alienating. Nevertheless, he is a lonely man whose shocking personal losses invite our sympathy and compassion. His situation ultimately strikes a chord with Leon and the two men share an uneasy alliance. John's admission that he *was* home on the night of Valerie's accident is not just for the benefit of Leon, the investigating cop. It is also a purging of self before an equally flawed individual who has also 'fucked up' (Sc.66a). The reasons behind John's lie underscore his claustrophobic sense of entrapment within the marriage. He feels suffocated, but short of leaving Valerie he has few options. It is clear that he does love her. But, equally, 'sometimes love isn't enough' (Sc.72).

Paula

Key Quotes

'If you ever fuck with our marriage, I'll cut your balls off – I'll hang them on the line between your socks and your jocks.' (Sc.45)
'He didn't do it Jane.' (Sc.87)

As a working mother with three young children, life is not easy for Paula. Her husband is unemployed and she carries considerable responsibility as the family breadwinner. She has taken on an extra shift at the hospital in order to bring more money into the household. Nevertheless, she is a contented woman, sustained by her own inner strength and a secure, loving relationship. When she tells Jane that she knows Nik had done nothing wrong, simply because 'he told me' (Sc.87), it sums up her absolute faith in her husband. She loves him unconditionally and is prepared to trust him without question. Paula is passionate about her marriage and expects the same commitment in return. She has no hesitation in emphasising this point with humour and bluntness. Her comment about hanging Nik's balls up with his socks and his jocks is also an oblique reference to the domestic scaffolding which underpins their marriage. Together, they have created a rock solid structure that cannot be undermined from the outside; the only thing that could really threaten it would be betrayal from within.

The most important priority in Paula's life is her family. Her role is that of nurturer, both in her capacity as nurse and mother. If her family is threatened in any way, she takes no prisoners. Her relationship with Jane is a case in point. While initially the two women enjoy an easy friendship – note Paula's use of the diminutive 'Janey' – the latter's evident desire to exploit her single status makes her something of a loose cannon from Paula's perspective. When Jane informs the police of Nik's suspicious behaviour on the night of Valerie's disappearance, Paula interprets it as a hostile act and reacts bitterly to the perceived disloyalty. The last straw is when she returns home after collecting her children to discover that Jane has tidied up her house. Her sense of violation and rage makes it impossible for her to appreciate the well-meaning gesture.

Nik

Key Quotes

'You're in deep shit, Nik. Your wife can't help you.' (Sc.78, Leon)
'I don't want to stop. It's late and I think Paula will be getting worried. But what do I do? The woman needs help. So I pull over.' (Sc.85b)

Nik D'Amato is a good-natured, easygoing individual who loves his wife dearly and enjoys his life, despite the fact that he is out of work and finances are tight. He is a loving and committed family man. He looks after the baby and continues job hunting while Paula works, and we often see him playing with his children. He maintains contact with his old work colleagues, meeting them regularly for a drink, and has a well-defined sense of loyalty to his neighbour, Pete, whom he regards as a 'mate'. He dislikes subterfuge and subsequently feels he is letting Pete down by not saying anything to him about Jane's affair.

Nik knows how lucky he is in his marriage and relies on Paula absolutely. When he is apprehended by the police and taken to the station, he responds like a caged animal, pacing the room in which he is being held, calling for her without a care about what listeners may think. He needs the reassurance of her love and strength. It is Nik's generosity that has got him into trouble. He does not want to stop when Valerie waves him down, but ignoring her plight is not an option. Moreover, despite the inconvenience, he is prepared to drive her home even though her house is completely out of his way. Why doesn't he report what he knows to the police? The hole he digs for himself is foolish but, from his perspective, understandable. Nik is the type that regards the authorities, including the police, as a necessary evil. He is comfortable with cutting a few corners, like drinking too much and then going out of his way to avoid the booze bus. The fact that he *has* had too much to drink suggests that he may not have been thinking as clearly as he needed to. Yet, after chasing Valerie through the scrub, he does intuitively recognise that he cannot dispel her fear: 'I thought that if I left her alone, then she'd stop being afraid of me' (Sc.85b). Simply leaving her and then disposing of her shoe seems like a reasonable option. By the time he hears of her disappearance on the news, he feels trapped: 'Who was going to believe me?' (Sc.85b).

Patrick

Key Quotes

'And he asked to see me again. I wasn't expecting that.' (Sc.15)
'I'm a respite from a marriage that's gotten too hard.' (Sc.41)
'Well, she's the therapist. I wasn't that focused on how she was.' (Sc.68)

Patrick Phelan is a client of Valerie's and his role, though comparatively small, is an important part in the jigsaw. Through him, we see Valerie's impassive professional facade begin to falter. Their consultations are increasingly uncomfortable. He is continually trying to 'test' her. She feels threatened by his provocative manner and what she interprets as personally directed insinuations. It is indicative of her emotional paranoia that she entertains the rather bizarre, and totally unfounded, suspicion that he may be having an affair with her own husband.

Though an unsympathetic character, Patrick is arguably more vulnerable than he appears. He is, after all, seeking therapy. (We might also consider why he attends Valerie's book launch.) His relationships are often superficial and he has few expectations. His cynicism cannot entirely mask the loneliness implicit in the stark description of his sex life: 'We went home and had sex. As you do. Well, some of us do' (Sc.15). Moreover, he seems defensive with regard to his sexuality and tries to make it an issue in his sessions with Valerie. When he does fall in love, the fact that the man comes 'encumbered' (Sc.15) is a bitter irony. Rather than be critical of his lover, he spitefully targets the wife, dismissing any suggestion that she may be a victim, and presenting himself as 'a respite' (Sc.41). By his own admission, Patrick sees intimate relations in adversarial terms. Love is 'a contest' (Sc.26) with winners and losers. The fact that his lover decides, in the end, to return to his own family, leaving Patrick alone once again, probably does nothing to dispel this jaundiced viewpoint.

THEMES & ISSUES

Love and Marriage

The questions posed by Valerie at the book launch, 'Can we believe in love? Feel safe in it?' (Sc.12) resonate through the text. There are no simple answers. The four relationships under scrutiny offer different perspectives on the conundrum that is marriage and highlight the proposition that there are as many different kinds of marriages as there are individuals in them. Although married heterosexual love is the key focus of the text, gay love is also referred to, albeit briefly.

Lantana explores the ephemeral nature of love and reinforces the notion that true commitment can only flourish in a context of selflessness and loyalty. The marriages that survive must evince these qualities. Sonja's decision to forgive Leon is partially about loving him. It's also about recognising that the whole they have created together is so much more than the sum of its parts. As a parent, it is impossible for her to think of herself in isolation or divorce herself from what is also in the interests of her sons. Leon's contrition and declaration that he needs her give her the strength to put aside her hurt pride and make a decision for the common good. 'Loving someone means we have to relinquish power. It's mutual surrender' (Sc.12). Both Sonja and Leon value profoundly the concept of family and, for them, it is built into the essence of their marriage. For example, Leon's almost pathological crusade against drugs is partially about protecting these interests; as a cop, he has had first-hand exposure to the way drugs can destroy young lives and families.

Equally, Paula and Nik's life together is based on the premise that their love for each other, and their kids, is the bastion that protects them against life's vicissitudes. When Jane tells Paula that she no longer loves Pete, Paula is silenced. She cannot imagine a marriage without love and she is not prepared to argue that anyone should stay in a marriage missing this fundamental ingredient. Believing in love, feeling safe, therefore becomes a self-fulfilling prophecy. Nik and Paula are representatives of the 'privileged few' (Sc.12) to whom Valerie refers. For them, 'home is a sanctuary' (Sc.12). Despite the problems Sonja and Leon face, they too belong to this select cohort. Their ability to make allowances for weakness, their willingness to compromise and work through issues, and the security offered to their children, affords them ultimate affiliation.

By contrast, the marriages of Valerie and John and Jane and Pete are 'a battleground' (Sc.12), though for different reasons. Valerie and John do, in fact, love each other. However, overshadowing their relationship is the legacy of their daughter's murder and their differing responses to it. When John tells Leon that sometimes love is not enough, this is not to suggest that it is lacking on his part. Nor should his contribution to the marriage be trivialised. John demonstrates his love for his wife, not in the way she would like, or even needs, but in the only way he is able. He is literally still there for her. The last thing that Valerie tells her husband is that she loves him. She concludes her message with 'Wait for me. We'll talk when I get home. I love you' (Sc.51). Like Sonja, Valerie wants 'emotional honesty' (Sc.10) and regards it as basic to a successful relationship. She holds on to this ideal; it is what sustains her through her doubt and grief and suspicion. We are not privy to the circumstances that have precipitated the breakdown of Jane and Pete's marriage; it may simply have run out of momentum. However, Pete is in the unenviable position of having had the decision made for him. He loves his estranged wife, but there appears little hope of reconciliation.

To date, homosexual love has not been endorsed by our society relative to heterosexual love. Gay men and lesbians have been marginalised at best, derided and discriminated against at worst. At the time of writing, conservative politicians have rejected the concept of gay marriage, despite the fact that this is being viewed as a legitimate option in some more liberal democracies overseas. This kind of discrimination may account for Patrick's defensiveness. At the same time, his bitter sense of grievance distorts his perspective. His reductionist view of love as a 'contest' (Sc.26), with its connotations of a power play and winning at any cost, is diametrically opposed to the suppression of ego that underpins other relationships in the text. Patrick's waspish appraisal of his lover's situation is that he 'comes encumbered' (Sc.15). The fact that the man returns to his wife is no doubt perceived by Patrick as a response to her 'manipulating' personality, rather than any loyalty, even love, his lover may feel towards her. Patrick is incapable of 'relinquishing power' (Sc.12) and, as such, is unlikely to find true or lasting romantic fulfilment.

Lantana concludes with another question, highlighted by the name of the song accompanying the final scenes – *Que Sabes Tu De Amor* (What Do You Know of Love?) What *do* any of us know? One thing that is apparent is the resilience of love; its capacity to forgive, to sustain trauma, and to rationalise hurt. Sonja's admission to Valerie that, despite everything, she does still love her husband encapsulates the tenacity and the pull of this most mercurial of emotions.

Trust

One of the key components in any relationship is trust. Valerie asserts that 'Trust is as vital to human relationships as breathing is to life' (Sc.12). She also notes its elusiveness. Trust is born out of honesty. If partners cannot, or will not, be honest with each other, then trust is compromised.

The extent to which individuals are capable of deceiving their partners, and indeed themselves, is raised within the context of Valerie's sessions with both Sonja and Patrick. Valerie actually makes the same point with regard to the situations each is in. Whether or not Leon is sensitive to his wife's unhappiness depends on 'how good an actor' (Sc.10) she is. Equally, the wife of Patrick's lover may not suspect his infidelity, depending on 'how good he is at deceiving her' (Sc.15). The onus is also on the partners to clue into their spouses' unhappiness. Sonja says rather desperately of her husband, 'I would have thought that maybe he wouldn't need to be told' (Sc.10). And Patrick argues that his lover's wife should recognise the reality of her husband's bisexuality: 'She would sense it…wouldn't she?'

(Sc.15). If not, he maintains it is because she willingly deludes herself through self-interest and emotional cowardice. A readiness to avoid facing the truth is one way, it is suggested, that some marriages survive. Patrick's cynicism leads him to conclude: 'There's knowing and there's knowing. Some women like to live the lie…it's easier than dealing with the truth' (Sc.26).

However, successful relationships are built on 'emotional honesty' (Sc.10). Sonja senses a lack of this in her relationship, even before she knows of Leon's adultery with Jane. Moreover, she admits to Valerie that she sees a lie as more damaging than the possibility of her husband having an affair: 'It's not that he might have slept with another woman. It's that he might not tell me. That would be the betrayal' (Sc.38). Given that this *is* the case, Leon will have to rebuild the trust that he has jeopardised. Valerie and John's situation demonstrates that this is not always easy. Valerie's relationship with her husband is fraught with ambivalence. She dedicates her book to him, 'For teaching me to trust again' (Sc.63). However, John himself divulges the fact that he has had an affair in the past and, as a result, 'something gets broken permanently – trust I suppose' (Sc.72). While he is disturbed that Valerie suspected him of having a relationship with Patrick Phelan, he is not as surprised or affronted as he might be: 'Anything's now possible, it would seem' (Sc.72).

Valerie's sense of security and ability to trust has been further destroyed by the murder of her child and she has become frightened and suspicious, seeing shadows everywhere. She misinterprets her husband's need for solitude and continues to cling to him, alienating him even further. Nevertheless, John admits to Leon that 'most men hold something back' (Sc.61b) and he deliberately refuses to share with Valerie his visits to the laneway where their daughter died. When Valerie's life depends on it and she most needs to trust, she cannot. Nik would have helped her, but she is so alarmed when he turns off the main road that she jumps out of the moving car. As she flees, terrified, through the scrub, he exhorts her to 'trust me' (Sc.85b) but she is incapable of believing him.

Conversely, Paula's faith in Nik counterbalances the lack of it being played out in the other relationships. Despite himself, Leon is touched by what he witnesses between the young couple. Paula trusts her husband absolutely and is prepared to accept what he says at face value. It is enough that he denies the charge against him; from her perspective, additional qualification or explanation is unnecessary. The solidarity and honesty that underpin their relationship enable them to effectively withstand any crisis that confronts them.

Yearning and Loss

Andrew Bovell has noted the 'undefined yearning' shared by a number of the key characters in the text. *Lantana* asks the questions, Who are we? What do we want to be? Why is there often such disparity between the two? It explores the challenge of retaining a sense of hope and optimism in the face of harsh realities. In particular, the text focuses on middle-aged angst and the frustrated expectations of the post-baby boom era. The realisation that life will not necessarily fulfil its anticipated promise, and the recognition that cherished aspirations may be increasingly unattainable pipedreams, is a confronting turning point for most.

In some instances, this disappointment relates specifically to the characters' personal relationships. Leon's sense that life is passing him by is such that he has lost the capacity to feel. This has resulted in him indulging in a casual marital infidelity that poses a threat to everything he holds dear. He loves his wife and wants to be a good father to his sons. Yet he finds himself increasingly desperate to do something, anything, that will reignite his passion for life – even if it means jeopardising the loyalty of those closest to him. The irony is that Sonja craves the same thing. She tells Valerie that she wants a relationship that is 'passionate' and 'challenging' (Sc.10). She does not want to preserve a facade for the sake of it, nor does she feel she can settle for second best if indeed Leon is unfaithful, even for the sake of her children. Leon seems oblivious to his wife's discontent and is shocked by the discovery that she has sought counselling: 'There was a time when there was no private between you and me' (Sc.64).

Neither Valerie nor John's needs are being met by their relationship. Valerie wants John to depend on her emotionally; she wants him to talk to her and share his grief, she wants to know what he's thinking. John's disillusionment is absolute; he has not come to terms with Eleanor's death and he simply wants to be left alone. Jane's 'high expectations' (Sc.31) have resulted in her leaving a man who loves her and generously continues to support her, regardless of the difficult position in which it places him. Jane is acutely conscious of time passing and is adamant with regard to moving on. She yearns for romance and is willing to reinvent herself in order to accommodate a new relationship. Her optimism makes her vulnerable. While she is being honest when she tells Leon that she is really attracted to him, she is also attracted by the possibility of a fresh start.

These characters are all 'searching for a sense of clarification in their emotional lives'.[9] They are preoccupied with what they have lost, or are losing. In some cases, their preoccupation is a comment on unrealistic expectations or an inability to recognise what they *do* have. For example, what Leon stands to lose through his adultery is much greater than what he thinks he has missed out on to date. Nevertheless, their loss of faith is also contextual. In her address, Valerie alludes to a pervasive disillusionment within society: 'the confused cry of the modern age' (Sc.12). She suggests that, as a community, we no longer know what to believe in. In Valerie's world, hope flounders, values are continually compromised, and cynicism prevails. Her profession – and her own bitter experience – has given her first-hand exposure to the downside of the human condition. She reiterates, 'It's not meant to be like that, but it is' (Sc.12). Ironically, the 'commercialisation' of her daughter's memory could be construed as symptomatic of the very erosion of values that she refers to in her speech.

The cruellest loss depicted in the text is the death of eleven-year-old Eleanor Knox. Losing a child under any circumstances is an irreconcilable grief; Eleanor's brutal abduction and murder is particularly traumatic for her parents to accept: 'This wasn't supposed to happen, but it did' (Sc.12). Both Valerie and John would give anything to turn the clock back. Valerie cannot look at a child without being reminded of what she has lost. Her pensive acknowledgment of a little girl in the street inevitably evokes memories of her own daughter. She asks her husband plaintively, and somewhat naively, 'Do you think about her very much?' (Sc.33). The answer is, of course, yes. The 'professional' Valerie would probably admit that there are different, and equally legitimate, ways to express grief. Hers is overt. She has published her book and is actively involved in its promotion. She lectures publicly on loss and, presumably, encourages her clients to articulate their feelings. For some personalities, however, the psychiatrist's stratagem of 'opening up' is counterproductive. John's

[9] Bovell, *Lantana* Screenplay, p.8.

response is to internalise, to compartmentalise the bereavement; this is what gets him through the day. Sadly, their divergent reactions to the tragedy have led to the further breakdown of intimacy in their marriage. What holds the relationship together is, in fact, grief: 'There wasn't much else left' (Sc.72).

Loyalty and Betrayal

Sonja's understandable sense of grievance against her husband when she discovers his adultery leads to her scornful value judgment: 'You know what's so easy Leon – it's so easy to go out and find somebody. You know what's hard – what's hard is not to' (Sc.66a). Leon, dissatisfied with his life and desperate to reclaim the ability to 'feel', has lied to Sonja and betrayed her faith in him. Yet, in talking to John, he quotes loyalty as one of the key elements in his marriage. It is debatable whether or not Leon has truly considered the ramifications of his actions. He admits to Jane that their relationship is not necessarily something he planned and rather ingenuously suggests that things between them 'do not have to end badly' (Sc.31). Sonja, on the other hand, has resisted the temptation to compromise her marriage and has a much more finely-tuned appreciation of the risks involved. Her decision to seek counselling demonstrates greater loyalty to herself and her family than Leon's self-indulgent 'resolution' of his problems.

Paula's unwavering loyalty to her husband has already been discussed. Her blunt response to the idea of Nik being unfaithful leaves no doubt that she demands the same commitment in return: 'If you ever fuck with our marriage, I'll cut your balls off' (Sc.45). While there is little likelihood of Nik even looking elsewhere, Paula *does* feel betrayed by what she interprets as Jane's treachery. How much choice does Jane have in reporting Nik's actions to the police? It is clear that she values Paula's friendship and regrets the decision she has to make. Nevertheless, it is difficult to imagine that the two women will resume their former closeness.

Are men more likely to be unfaithful than women? There are at least two examples of males cheating on their wives proffered in the text, with Leon and John sharing this dubious affiliation. However, in addition to Nik's loyalty to Paula, Pete's devotion to Jane is presented as a deliberate foil to Leon's behaviour. Here the marital roles are reversed, with Jane desperate to recapture a slice of her youth and prepared to do whatever it takes to further her 'potential', including off-loading her partner of many years.

The text also invites us to speculate about the difference between genuine loyalty and an unwillingness to take risks. Sometimes it is simply easier to preserve the status quo, but this might be counterproductive. John has demonstrated tenacious loyalty to Valerie after the death of their daughter. He is unhappy in his marriage, but has stood by his wife, unable to bring himself to leave a woman who is in so much pain herself. In hindsight, is this wise, or even fair? We are reminded of the dialogue between Valerie and Patrick regarding the reasons why people stay in a relationship that, arguably, is past its use-by date. Valerie maintains that 'good men don't know how to leave their wives'. Patrick counters, 'Good men or cowardly men?' (Sc.41).

John's decision to stay in his marriage has heartbreaking consequences and leads ultimately to betrayal. In remaining with Valerie, John feels smothered by her emotional demands. He is unable to respond in the way she wants him to and, on occasions, he specifically rejects her pleas for emotional reassurance. It is possible he is suffering from depression. Deliberately ignoring her phone calls on the night of the accident is part of a broader framework of resentment and suppressed anger. He *knows* that Valerie is afraid of being alone, yet he chooses to disregard the fact that she is stranded on a deserted road, late at night. While it is unclear at what point he did come home, and when exactly he accessed all of her messages, the inference is that he *was* there the whole time. John tells Leon that he 'thought she would come home' (Sc.89) and there is no reason to doubt his sincerity. However, the miscalculation and its consequences will haunt him. He will have to live with this betrayal of trust for the rest of his life and the knowledge that, had he responded to her need, Valerie's death may have been prevented.

QUESTIONS & ANSWERS

The text response questions on the examination paper are divided into two groups. Each requires a different approach. The first group requires an interpretive response to the text and focuses on characters, relationships, style, structure and narrative. The second group calls for a discussion of the themes and issues, values, social perspectives and the unstated views that texts may embody through their representations of people, events, issues and ideas. These questions relate to the wider implications of the text.

Part 1 Questions

1 'She's very needy.'

'The characters in Lantana are both compromised and empowered by their dependence on each other.' Discuss.

2 'Leon is an aggressive cop and an unfaithful husband, yet he retains our sympathy.' How does the film win our support for Leon?

3 'Valerie and John are at an impossible crossroads in their marriage.' Do you agree?

4 *Lantana* is both a drama about relationships and a police mystery. How does the filmmaker reconcile these two elements?

5 '…because he told me.'

'While Paula's faith in her husband is touching, it is also rather naive.' Do you agree?

Part 2 Questions

1 'Sometimes love isn't enough.'

'*Lantana* suggests that love is only one element in a successful marriage.' Discuss.

2 'Don't you ever want to cry sometimes?'

What conclusions does the text draw about men's responses to stress?

3 '*Lantana* explores the way in which love triumphs over betrayal.' Discuss.

4 'Trust is as vital to human relationships as breathing is to life – and just as elusive.'

How does *Lantana* explore the fragile nature of trust?

5 'While *Lantana* is both written and directed by men, it explores the emotional needs of women with great precision.' Discuss.

Analysing a Sample Topic

1 'She's very needy.'

'The characters in *Lantana* are both compromised and empowered by their dependence on each other.' Discuss.

- The key words here are 'compromised', 'empowered' and 'dependence'. This question invites you to analyse the way in which the need that underpins most relationships can be both a positive and a negative quality, and the extent to which it can undermine the individuals concerned, or invigorate and fortify them. Given that an acknowledgment of the complexities of the issue is built into the topic, it would be advisable to agree with the statement and develop your contention accordingly. Remember, your introduction is vital. Make your stance clear and indicate your line of argument.
- Identify the opening quotation. To whom does it refer? Patrick's disparaging remarks about his lover's wife are a way of deflecting his own responsibility in the love triangle. In this context, the wife's dependence is portrayed as selfish and manipulative. If this is true, then presumably it compromises both her and her husband. Given that Valerie identifies strongly with the wife's situation as she listens, you will need to examine Valerie's own relationship with John. Is Valerie too dependent? What has made her this way? How does she demonstrate this need and what is John's reaction? Does he depend on her at all? What is the long-term effect on the couple of the unhappy power play that seems to characterise their marriage?
- Are there other examples in the text of a dependency that compromises the individuals concerned? At what point does loyalty merge into unhealthy reliance? Consider Pete's dilemma. He wants to be supportive to the woman he still loves, but runs the risk of being exploited by Jane, whose own need of an accommodating presence seems entirely contingent on expediency.
- Remember, this particular topic has two parts. It suggests that dependence is a two-sided coin. Do not make the (common) mistake of concentrating too exclusively on one aspect of the question.

- The best illustration of characters being empowered by their mutual dependence is Nik and Paula. The crisis that they face highlights the strength and resilience that is such a feature of their relationship. Where does this strength come from? How does it manifest itself? What general lessons can be extrapolated from their example?
- Ironically, it is often by having a strong sense of self that we are able to acknowledge our dependence on others. Evaluate Sonja and Leon's situation. Sonja's love for her husband and her children, and the recognition that she cannot be truly content without them, enable her to forgive Leon's duplicity. Equally, he concedes that his happiness is inextricably bound with hers.
- Note that *Lantana* is a non-print text and you are expected to make reference to the way in which cinematic techniques support meaning. For example, it would be appropriate to comment on the use of close-ups to highlight Valerie's desperate bid to force intimacy with her husband.
- To need others is a fundamental part of the human psyche. If we open ourselves up to different relationships, then we make ourselves vulnerable. In some cases, this can be disabling. Alternatively, depending on the context and the personalities, as well as the qualities that are brought to each relationship, individuals may be empowered by their dependence on others. Your answer must 'unpack' the complexities embedded in the question. You may have to be selective – you will be writing your response under time constraints – but you must address as many relevant aspects as possible. Consider the broader social implications of the topic statement, but support general observations with detailed reference to the text. In your conclusion, restate the contention, tie the threads of your argument together, and sum up your position economically and succinctly.

REFERENCES & READING

Text

Lantana, Dir. Ray Lawrence, Twentieth Century Fox, 2001.

Further Reading

Bovell, Andrew, *Lantana* Screenplay, Currency Press, Sydney, 2001.

Beal, Melanie, *Lantana: A Journey through the Labyrinth of Life,* Australian Screen Education, Issue 34, Autumn, 2004.

Websites

http://www.palace.net.au/lantana/index.htm

http://www.hollywood.com/movies/detail/movie/416112

http://www.beyond.com.au/pdfs/lantana.pdf

http://www.tiscali.co.uk/entertainment/film/reviews/lantana.html

Other Titles in this Series

A Lesson Before Dying
A View from the Bridge
Angela's Ashes
Blade Runner
Border Crossing
Breaker Morant
Brilliant Lies
Cabaret
Cloudstreet
Dead Letter Office
Diving for Pearls
Dream Stuff
Falling
First They Killed Father
Fly Away Peter
Gattaca
Girl with a Pearl Earring
Going Home
Hamlet
Henry Lawson's Short Stories
I for Isobel
If This is a Man
I'm Not Scared
In the Lake of the Woods
Jackson's Track
Lantana
Life of Galileo
Maestro
Macbeth
Medea
Minimum of Two
Montana 1948
Night
No Great Mischief
Oedipus the King
One True Thing
Only the Heart
Othello
Romulus, My Father
Shakespeare in Love
Stolen
Tess of the D'Urbervilles
The Age of Innocence
The Chant of Jimmie Blacksmith
The Curious Incident of the Dog in the Night-time
The Divine Wind
The Freedom of the City
The Great Gatsby
The Hunter
The Longest Memory
The Outsider
The Penguin Book of WW1 Poetry
The Plague
The Player
The Quiet American
The Stories of Tobias Wolff
The Things They Carried
The Third Man
The Wife of Martin Guerre
The Year of Living Dangerously
Things Fall Apart
Triage
What's Eating Gilbert Grape?